BEST BULBS
for the PRAIRIES

BEST BULBS
for the PRAIRIES

Liesbeth Leatherbarrow and Lesley Reynolds

Illustrations by Grace Buzik

FIFTH
HOUSE

The publisher gratefully acknowledges the support of The Canada Council for the Arts and the Department of Canadian Heritage.

THE CANADA COUNCIL | LE CONSEIL DES ARTS
FOR THE ARTS | DU CANADA
SINCE 1957 | DEPUIS 1957

We acknowledge the financial support of the Government of Canada through the Book Publishing Industry Development Program for our publishing activities.

Printed in Canada
01 02 03 04 05/ 5 4 3 2 1

CANADIAN CATALOGUING IN PUBLICATION DATA

Leatherbarrow, Liesbeth.
  Best bulbs for the prairies

  Includes index.
  ISBN 1-894004-61-2

  1. Bulbs—Prairie Provinces. I. Reynolds, Lesley. II. Title.
SB425.L42 2001   635.9'4'09712   C00–911409–2

Front cover image by Liesbeth Leatherbarrow
Back cover image by Lesley Reynolds
Interior illustrations by Grace Buzik
Design by Thinkinc Communications Ltd.

Published in Canada by
Fifth House Ltd.
A Fitzhenry & Whiteside Company
1511–1800 4 Street SW
Calgary, Alberta, Canada
T2S 2S5

Published in the U.S. by
Fitzhenry & Whiteside
121 Harvard Ave.
Suite 2
Allston, Massachusetts
01234

Table of Contents

Foreword

The bright pictures in mail-order catalogues and on packaged bulbs in retail outlets almost always provide gardeners with the incentive to purchase bulbs. But given the worldwide market, these pictures and their descriptions seldom supply enough information for growing these plants on the North American prairies. Is a particular bulb hardy or tender? Does it flourish in sun or shade? In which type of soil is it likely to give its best performance? What sort of life expectancy should you assume? Finding this information has been a somewhat daunting task in the past; not finding it leaves prairie gardeners ill-equipped to give bulbs their best effort.

Best Bulbs for the Prairies, by Liesbeth Leatherbarrow and Lesley Reynolds, provides prairie gardeners with the answers they need to grow beautiful plants from bulbs. Not only have the authors grown these bulbs in their own gardens, but they have also sought out the successes (and failures) of other gardeners across the prairies. They have coupled their empirical knowledge with well-researched history on the origin and introduction of these bulbs, their early uses, and the folklore associated with them. As well as being a cornucopia of information, the book is lovingly illustrated with clear, full-colour photographs by the authors juxtaposed with delicate line drawings by Calgarian Grace Buzik.

Best Bulbs for the Prairies is both an invitation to the tried and tested and an incentive to explore the microclimates of your own landscape to expand the ever-increasing possibilities of bulbs that can be grown on the prairies. It covers a wide range, from tender tropical summer bulbs to tough and hardy species from central Asia. It provides consumer information on what to look for at the point of purchase, warnings on endangered bulbs collected from the wild, and cultural practices geared to multiplying your bulbs.

Learning is a good thing, for the more you know, the more successful you are likely to be. And, certainly, you can learn a lot from this book. The authors lead beginning gardeners through the basics, while offering those with more experience a wealth of rare, unusual, and often sadly under-used bulbs, both hardy and tender, that are perfect for the prairies given the proper conditions. In short, *Best Bulbs for the Prairies* gives all gardeners the encouragement and the knowledge to succeed.

Sara Williams, Editor, The Gardener for the Prairies
Horticultural Specialist, Extension Division
University of Saskatchewan, November 2000

Acknowledgments

Books, especially gardening books, are never written in isolation, and several friends, and even a few strangers, have had a hand in our book. From sharing horticultural expertise to welcoming us into their private gardens to take photos, from lending us slides from personal collections to giving us much-needed encouragement and moral support—our gardening friends have done all this for us, and more. To everyone who contributed to this project, we give our heartfelt thanks.

In particular, we'd like to thank our correspondents from Saskatchewan and Manitoba. They completed our bulb questionnaires, sharing their favorite bulb species and cultivars, and confirmed that prairie gardeners experience the same joys and challenges when it comes to growing bulbs no matter where they live on the prairies.

Special thanks are due to Rod Shaver and Llyn Strelau, extraordinary plantsmen with an equally extraordinary garden. Their amazing and diverse plant collection proves that you can't always believe what books say about plant hardiness. We spent many pleasant hours with them last spring and summer, chatting and photographing their unusual and specialized bulbs. Llyn also kindly loaned us slides for inclusion in the book.

We'd like to send another special thank you to Lori Skulski and Stuart Dechka for allowing us to photograph their wonderful spring-flowering bulb collection. Astounding in both size and variety, their lavish bulb display presents a continuous kaleidoscope of color from early April until late June and is a fine example of how to extend the growing season on the prairies.

No gardening book deserves a place on a bookstore shelf until it has been given the stamp of approval by critical readers. Our readers—Susanna Barlem (Ornamental Gardener/Propagator, Calgary Zoo Botanical Gardens, Calgary), Chris Biesheuvel (recently retired Horticultural Development Manager, A. E. McKenzie Co. Inc., Brandon), Ken Girard (Greenhouse Manager, Department of Biological Sciences, University of Calgary, Calgary), and Wendy Mackie (Horticulture Coordinator, Assiniboine Park Conservatory, Winnipeg)—took time from their busy lives to read our manuscript and we thank them for their efforts. Our book has benefited considerably from their thoughtful suggestions and guidance. Ken also generously gave us access to his slide collection.

Grace Buzik, an amazing artist, talented graphic designer, and good friend, created the beautiful line drawings that dot the pages of this book. Her ability to capture our botanical themes with her signature style is remarkable.

As always, it has been a pleasure to work with our friends at Fifth House Publishers. From the day the bulb project was conceived, Fraser Seely, Charlene Dobmeier, Catherine Radimer, and Kathy Bogusky have encouraged us and guided us through the publishing process once again. Also, we were delighted when Charlene invited Geri Rowlatt to edit our manuscript. Geri's eagle eye, attention to detail, and language skills are second to none.

Finally, this book could not have been written without the unconditional support of our families. We owe Camille, Kate, Vic, and Bob a lifetime of hugs and kisses for their patience and understanding.

1Introduction

Planting spring-flowering bulbs in the fall is a gift gardeners give to themselves. There is no better way to achieve a beautiful spring garden on the prairies, where gardeners are often limited by the short growing season. Early-blooming treasures such as heavenly blue Siberian squill and petite white snowdrops are in many ways the most precious flowers of the gardening year. Their emergence is always cause for celebration of the approach of the new growing season, and is accompanied by a sense of wonder that such fragile-looking flowers can survive in the blustery and cold early prairie spring. And what could be more versatile than the tulip? Literally thousands of tulip cultivars are on the market in a spectacular array of colors and forms; choose wisely and you can have a succession of gorgeous tulips in your prairie garden for almost three months. Most of the spring-flowering bulbs recommended in this book are extremely hardy, scorning subzero temperatures and heavy snowfall. Many years, for instance, *Iris reticulata* is bravely blooming in our gardens by the end of March.

However, it doesn't end there—summer- and fall-blooming bulbs are available to take gardeners through the growing season in style. Hardy lilies (including new ones bred on the prairies) and alliums are staples of the summer border; autumn crocus and *Colchicum* make surprise entries when everything else is winding down in the fall. In addition, there is a host of tender bulbs, from *Agapanthus* to *Zephyranthes*, to bring a touch of tropical elegance to warm summer evenings in the garden.

Masses of brilliant pink 'Barcelona' Triumph tulips are spectacular against a background of pink and white flowering ornamental crabapples and spirea. *Liesbeth Leatherbarrow*

1

Bulbs are found all over the world, but most favorite hardy bulbs come from areas with a Mediterranean climate—hot, dry summers and cool, wet winters. This type of climate prevails in southern Europe, northwest Africa, Asia Minor, and parts of Asia, where tulips, crocus, narcissus, grape hyacinth, squill, and hyacinth originate. In certain areas within this region, particularly the mountainous terrain of Turkey, Iran, and Russia, winters are very cold and snowy. The climate is, in fact, not unlike that of the prairies, and the floral natives of these regions settle into our gardens comfortably.

Other bulbs originate in places with cold winters and warm, wet summers, such as parts of Europe and eastern North America. Many of our favorite woodland species, including trillium, dog's-tooth violet, and Jack-in-the-pulpit, fall into this category and require extra summer moisture. Two of our most popular bulbs are widely distributed throughout the northern hemisphere: irises and lilies are versatile genera found in many habitats in Europe, North America, and Asia.

More bulbs are native to South Africa than anywhere else in the world. Depending on the area they come from, they are adapted either to a wet winter/dry summer Mediterranean climate or to wet summers and dry winters. Other bulbs come from moist and humid tropical regions of Africa, Asia, and the Americas. Naturally, no bulbs from these regions survive a prairie winter, but they are splendid summer-flowering bulbs or houseplants.

When you choose to add flowering bulbs to your gardens, you are following in the footsteps of the ancients. Lilies are depicted on five-thousand-year-old Sumerian tablets, frescoes of crocuses, lilies, and irises decorated the palace walls at Knossos, Crete, in 1500 BC, and anemones, irises, lilies, and narcissus were all represented in ancient Egyptian art. The Greek philosopher Theophrastus mentions anemone, crocus, gladiola, grape hyacinth, lily, narcissus, ranunculus, and squill in writings dating to 340 BC. And let's not overlook the Greek and Roman myths, rife with flowering bulbs springing up from the blood of dead heroes and beautiful youths, myths that have their origin in the annual ritual of death and rebirth, an apt metaphor for spring-flowering bulbs.

Of course, the most famous event in bulb history, the Dutch tulip craze of the seventeenth century, led to the eventual establishment of the Netherlands as the home of the leading bulb growers and hybridizers in the world.

No matter where you live on the prairies, there are bulbs to suit your particular little garden paradise. Do yourself a favor by making bulb planting part of your gardening ritual. You'll thank yourself in the spring!

2 What are Bulbs?

Undoubtedly, true bulbs and their close relatives comprise one of nature's evolutionary wonders. Not only do they add beauty, grace, and style to the garden, they also come equipped with their very own custom-grown food supply. Completely self-reliant, with their favorite meals safely stowed in a swollen underground storage system, what could be easier than bulbs for a gardener to grow? Planted properly and in the right location, healthy bulbs are a guaranteed success in prairie gardens.

Bulbs for the prairies are described either as hardy or tender, depending on their ability to survive our harsh winters. Hardy bulbs are the survivors, reappearing every year in ever larger, showier clusters, despite the bitter cold. In fact, hardy bulbs require a cold spell to strut their stuff the following year. Tender bulbs, however, do not survive our winters underground and must be lifted and stored for the duration, only to be replanted outdoors again in spring. Lifting and storing is a daunting prospect for some gardeners; luckily, most tender bulbs are sufficiently inexpensive that they can be treated as annuals and bought anew every spring. Their undeniably exotic look and often luxurious fragrance make them well worth the effort or the money, whichever you have in good supply.

Most of us use the word "bulb" indiscriminately (and incorrectly) to describe five distinct types of underground growth and storage structures—each with its own characteristics—true bulbs, corms, tubers, rhizomes, and tuberous roots. The technical name for such plants is geophyte, but because the term is unfamiliar to most of us, popular usage of the word "bulb" is adhered to in this book. In addition, true bulbs are designated as such.

All bulbs contain energy reserves to help them grow rapidly when conditions are favorable and to survive when they are not. Many bulbs are equipped to survive extreme drought, extreme cold, or both. However, their configuration and growth patterns (cycles) differ and are worth understanding so they can be given optimum growing conditions in the garden.

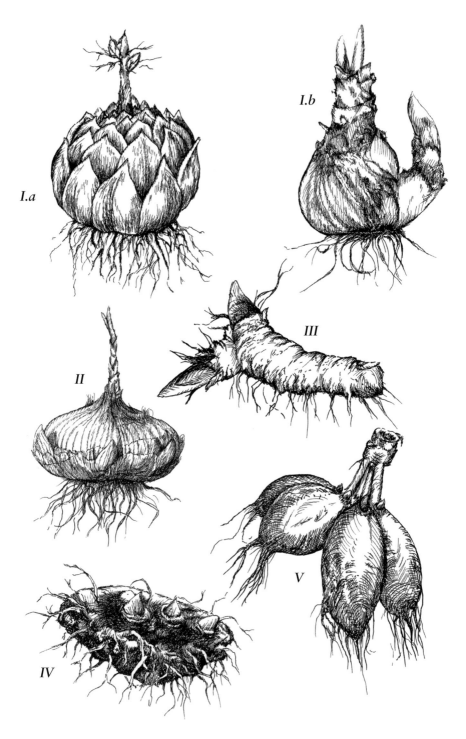

BULB TYPES I. True Bulb: (a) *Lilium* (lily) (b) *Narcissus* (daffodil) II. Corm: *Crocus* III. Rhizome: *Iris*
IV. Tuber: *Begonia* V. Tuberous Root: *Dahlia*

True Bulbs

When asked to describe a bulb, the image that comes to the average gardener's mind is usually that of a true bulb (e.g., onion)—a round, oval, or pear-shaped bundle of concentric, fleshy scales that come to a point at the top. They are often covered with a smooth, brown, papery skin called a tunic, which protects them against injury and dehydration. True bulbs without a tunic, such as lilies, must be handled with care to prevent damage and should be planted quickly to avoid shriveling and drying.

A true bulb is an underground stem base, and its scales are actually a series of modified leaves, held together at the bottom by a basal plate. The scales contain all the food necessary to nourish the plant during dormancy and an initial growth spurt. These can be loosely arranged (as with lilies and fritillarias) or very tightly wrapped, giving an almost solid appearance (as with daffodils and tulips). If you cut a true bulb in half horizontally, the scales look like a series of concentric rings. A true bulb's roots sprout from the bottom of the basal plate.

At the time of planting, true bulbs already contain tiny, undeveloped plants deep within the scales' protection, complete with stems, leaves, and flower buds.

Growth Cycle of a Spring-flowering Hardy Bulb

Autumn
- Bulbs/corms, complete with an embryonic plant, are planted in a dormant state.
- Cool temperatures and adequate moisture trigger root growth from the basal plate.
- Plant shoots start to grow from deep within the bulb.
- The bulb is nourished by stored nutrients.

Winter
- Plant shoot tips hover just below the soil's surface.
- Roots may stop growing.

Spring
- With rising temperatures, roots resume downward growth.
- Plant shoots break the soil's surface.
- Leaves grow vigorously.
- Flower buds swell.
- Bulbs start to produce offsets.
- Bulbs still rely on stored nutrients.

Spring/Early Summer
- Bulb foliage reaches mature size.
- Bulbs produce flowers.
- Flowers are pollinated.
- Stored energy reserves are depleted by this time.
- Offsets continue to grow.

Summer
- Flowers fade and non-sterile types set seed.
- Leaves continue to grow and function, replenishing the stored food supply through photosynthesis.
- Embryonic plants, harboring next year's flowers, develop deep within the replenished bulb.
- Leaves fade, wither, and die.
- Main bulb and offsets enter dormant phase.
- Bulbs may be left in place or lifted, cleaned, and stored in a cool, dry place until planting time in autumn.

'CP152' and 'Sun Ray' lilies grow from true bulbs. *Liesbeth Leatherbarrow*

True bulbs multiply by forming buds around the lower edges of the scales, which, in turn, develop into bulblets or offsets during the growing season. With some true bulbs, such as daffodils, the mother bulb continues to grow happily, even as her offspring are maturing and producing blossoms of their own. However, with other true bulbs such as tulips and ornamental onions, the mother bulb gives up the ghost after flowering, shriveling to nothing, and is replaced by bulblets of varying sizes. The largest of these bulblets usually bloom the following year; smaller ones may take several years to flower.

Tulips, daffodils, snowdrops, hyacinths, and ornamental onions are all good examples of true bulbs.

Growth Cycle of a Fall-flowering Hardy Bulb

Autumn
- Bulbs/corms, complete with an embryonic plant, are planted in a dormant state.
- Cool temperatures and adequate moisture immediately trigger root growth from the basal plate.
- Plant shoots start to grow, rapidly producing bare stems topped by flower buds.
- Buds burst into bloom within days.
- Flowers are pollinated.
- Stored nutrient supply is partially depleted.

Winter
- Bulbs enter a period of dormancy.

Spring
- With rising temperatures, roots resume downward growth.
- Plant shoots break the soil's surface.
- Leaves grow vigorously.
- Seeds are set for flowers pollinated in the fall.
- Bulbs start to produce offsets.
- Stored energy reserves are depleted by this time.

Summer
- Leaves continue to grow and function, replenishing the stored food supply through photosynthesis.
- Embryonic plants, harboring next year's flowers, develop deep within the replenished bulb.
- Leaves fade, wither, and die.
- Main bulb and offsets enter dormant phase.
- Bulbs may be left in place or lifted, cleaned, and stored in a cool, dry place until planting time in autumn.

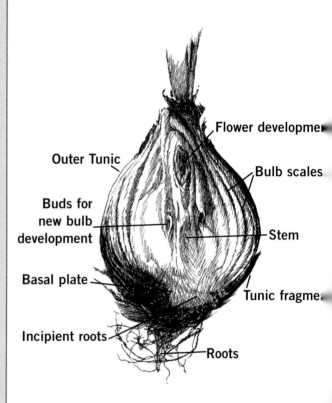

Flower development
Outer Tunic
Bulb scales
Buds for new bulb development
Stem
Basal plate
Tunic fragment
Incipient roots
Roots

Like all true bulbs, tulip bulbs contain tiny, undeveloped plants, complete with stems, leaves, and flower buds, protected by concentric, fleshy scales that contain enough food to nourish the plant through dormancy and initial growth.

Corms

Corms are modified underground stems, swollen with stored nutrients. It is easy to mistake a corm for a true bulb because they look alike, but there are some distinct differences.

- Corms are slightly flattened at the top—not pointed like true bulbs.
- Corms are protected on the outside by a fibrous or netted tunic rather than the relatively smooth tunic of true bulbs.
- Corms have a solid interior instead of the fleshy scales of true bulbs.

A basal plate defines the bottom of a corm and marks the spot where roots emerge. One or more growth points are found on corm tops. These growth points develop into the stems, leaves, and flower buds of plants.

A corm only lasts for one season. As its energy supply is depleted during the process of growing and blooming, it is replaced from the top by one or more daughter corms. These new corms may themselves produce several small offsets around the basal plate. These offsets, called cormels, eventually develop into productive plants.

Crocus, autumn crocus (*Colchicum*), freesia, and gladiola are typical corms.

Growth Cycle of a Summer-flowering Tender Bulb

Spring
- Bulbs are planted in warm soil (minimum 15.5° C, 60° F) when risk of hard frost has passed.
- Plant shoots break the soil's surface.
- Leaves begin to grow vigorously.
- Bulbs start to produce offsets.
- Bulbs still rely on stored nutrients.

Summer
- Bulb foliage reaches mature size.
- Bulbs produce flowers.
- Stored energy reserves are depleted by this time.
- Offsets continue to grow.
- Flowers fade and non-sterile types set seed.

Autumn
- Leaves continue to grow and function, replenishing the stored food supply through photosynthesis.
- Embryonic plants, harboring next year's flowers, develop deep within the replenished bulb.
- Leaves fade, wither, and die.
- Main bulb and offsets enter dormant phase.
- Bulbs must be lifted, cleaned, and stored indoors in a cool dry place until planting time the following spring.

Tubers

Like corms, tubers are solid underground stems, bulging with stored nutrients. They even look a bit like big corms, but are more irregular in shape and lack their basal plate and tunic. A tuber's surface is scattered with growth points, called eyes, which eventually develop into plant shoots on the upper side and the roots down below. The familiar potato is a good example of a tuber.

Crocus vernus 'Yellow Mammoth', 'Purpureus Grandiflorus', and 'Striped Beauty' grow from corms. *Liesbeth Leatherbarrow*

Some tubers, such as caladium, dwindle in size during the summer; at the same time, new replacement tubers or offsets develop at some growth points. Other tubers, such as begonias, continue to enlarge throughout the growing season, developing new growth points as they go, never producing any offsets.

Some anemones, begonias, and corydalis grow from tubers.

Rhizomes

Rhizomes are yet another example of thickened underground stems that serve as a storage organ for plant nutrients; they are solid like corms and tubers, but have neither a basal plate nor a tunic. Rhizomes cannot be lifted, dried, and stored aboveground for an extended period of time, unlike true bulbs, corms, and tubers. A familiar rhizome in the kitchen is gingerroot.

Rhizomes usually grow horizontally, at or below the soil's surface, forming small colonies with relative ease. They can be very rigid, thick, and fleshy, like bearded iris, or thin and wiry, like lily-of-the-valley. As developing rhizomes grow and divide along the way, older portions may wither and die. Rhizomes are sometimes called stem tubers.

A rhizome's root system develops on its undersides, and even though the primary growth point occurs at its leading edge (encased in scale-like leaves), many secondary growth points also develop at intervals along its length. These growth points can be found on the top surface of the rhizome and eventually develop into stems, leaves, and blossoms.

Bearded iris, canna, and lily-of-the-valley are good examples of plants that grow from rhizomes.

Tuberous Roots

Unlike true bulbs, corms, tubers, and rhizomes, which are all specialized stems, tuberous roots have their origin in root tissue that has been modified for food storage. The swollen roots usually radiate from a central point called the crown. Growth points, which give rise to stems, leaves, and blossoms, may be found nestled in the crown or on the bases of old stems that sprouted from the crown.

Once planted, tuberous roots sprout a network of ordinary fibrous roots all over their surface to look after the uptake of water and nutrients during the growing season.

Dahlias and foxtail lilies are examples of plants that grow from tuberous roots.

What Kind of Bulb Do You Have?

Note: *Plants that appear in more than one list come in more than one form.*

True Bulb
Allium (ornamental onion)
Camassia (camass)
Chionodoxa (glory-of-the-snow)
Crinum (crinum lily)
Eucomis (pineapple flower)
Fritillaria (fritillary)
Galanthus (snowdrop)
Galtonia (summer hyacinth)
Hyacinthoides (bluebell)
Hyacinthus (hyacinth)
Hymenocallis (spider lily)
Iris (iris)
Ixiolirion (ixia lily)
Leucojum (snowflake)
Lilium (lily)
Muscari (grape hyacinth)
Narcissus (daffodil)
Nectaroscordum (nectaroscordum)
Nerine (Guernsey lily)
Ornithogalum (star-of-Bethlehem)
Oxalis (wood sorrel)
Puschkinia (striped squill)
Scilla (squill)
Tigridia (tiger flower)
Tulipa (tulip)
Zephyranthes (fairy lily)

Corm
Babiana (baboon flower)
Bulbocodium (spring meadow saffron)
Colchicum (autumn crocus)
Crocosmia (montbretia)
Crocus (crocus)
Erythronium (dog's-tooth violet)
Freesia (freesia)
Gladiolus (gladiola)
Liatris (gayfeather)
Sparaxis (harlequin flower)
Triteleia (triteleia)
Tritonia (flame freesia)
Watsonia (bugle lily)

Tuber
Anemone blanda, A. coronaria (windflower)
Anemonella (rue anemone)
Arisaema (Jack-in-the-pulpit)
Begonia (tuberous begonia)
Caladium (fancy-leaved caladium)
Corydalis (tuberous corydalis)
Eranthis (winter aconite)
Oxalis (wood sorrel)
Ranunculus (Persian buttercup)

Rhizome
Agapanthus (lily-of-the-Nile)
Alstroemeria (Peruvian lily)
*Anemone canadensis,
    A. nemorosa,
    A. ranunculoides* (windflower)
Canna (canna)
Convallaria (lily-of-the-valley)
Iris (iris)
Oxalis (wood sorrel)
Sanguinaria (bloodroot)
Trillium (wakerobin)
Zantedeschia (calla lily)

Tuberous Root
Alstroemeria (Peruvian lily)
Dahlia (dahlia)
Eremurus (foxtail lily)
Liatris (gayfeather)

3 Landscaping with Bulbs

Every prairie garden, large or small, has a place for bulbs. Bulbs brighten flower beds, perennial and shrub borders, and foundation plantings. Early spring-flowering bulbs are dainty companions to alpine treasures in a rock garden, and provide unexpected patches of color in a lawn or peeking through a groundcover. Bulbs are at home under deciduous trees, in grassy meadows, or in front of fences or hedges. Weave an enticing ribbon of bulbs along a pathway or between stepping stones, or plant a patch of spring beside your front or back door. Later in the season, summer-flowering bulbs in containers are elegant additions to deck or patio gardens.

Whether your gardening style is formal and precise or informal and spontaneous, bulbs add color, fragrance, and sheer beauty to your garden in spring, summer, and fall. Formal plantings of boldly colored tulips contrast with the blue prairie sky, a welcome sight for winter-weary gardeners. Dreamy narcissus in soft yellow tones and dainty squill in the purest of blues create an enchanted setting of spring romance, especially when planted in drifts in a woodland or cottage-garden setting.

Color

Every gardener has favorite colors, and fortunately bulbs come in a range of hues from white to near black. The earliest spring blooms—bulbous irises, crocuses, squill, and snowdrops—tend to be in shades of blue, yellow, and white, followed by the bolder and more dramatic shades of tulips, and finally by the rich tropical-hued blooms of many summer-flowering bulbs.

Choose whichever colors please you most, but consider these guidelines.

- Before you purchase bulbs, decide on a color scheme. Group plants by color according to bloom time.
- Think about which colors show up best against fences, buildings, and trees and shrubs, especially evergreens.
- Limit each area to no more than three colors.

- Double Early yellow tulips 'Monte Carlo' with blue grape hyacinth (*Muscari armeniacum*)
- dwarf narcissus with blue grape hyacinth (*Muscari armeniacum*) and blue glory-of-the-snow (*Chionodoxa luciliae*)
- blue Siberian squill (*Scilla sibirica*) with *Crocus chrysanthus* 'Cream Beauty'
- mixed-color crocuses with *Tulipa kaufmanniana* 'Scarlet Baby'
- orange Triumph tulips 'Prinses Irene' and blue grape hyacinth (*Muscari armeniacum*) (see photo p. 13)
- purple, yellow, and white crocuses (see photo p. 8)
- pale yellow Large-cupped narcissus 'Ice Follies' with early *Tulipa fosteriana* 'Red Emperor'
- pink and white Large-cupped narcissus 'Accent' with salmon pink *Tulipa greigii* 'Toronto'
- purple veronica (*Veronica spicata*) and coral pink lilies (see photo p. 13)
- red *Tulipa kaufmanniana* 'Showwinner' and *Crocus vernus* 'Sky Blue'
- yellow narcissus and pink drumstick primula (*Primula denticulata*) (see photo p. 13)
- yellow auricula primula (*Primula auricula*) and blue grape hyacinth (*Muscari armeniacum*) (see photo p. 13)
- yellow cypress spurge (*Euphorbia cyparissias* 'Fens Ruby') with red *Tulipa linifolia* (see photo p. 13)
- yellow miniature narcissus 'Tête à Tête' with grape hyacinth (*Muscari armeniacum* 'Blue Spike')
- yellow Trumpet narcissus with red *Tulipa kaufmanniana* 'Showwinner' or *T. greigii* 'Red Riding Hood'
- Lily-flowered tulip 'White Triumphator' with purplish black Single Late tulip 'Queen of Night'
- yellow potentilla with red, yellow, or orange Asiatic lilies
- white Asiatic lilies with blue delphiniums

- Light colors, blue, purple, and soft pink shades look best in a partly shaded area, whereas reds, strong yellows, and oranges shine in sunny locations.
- Choose white-flowering bulbs to enhance color and to separate pastel shades from bright, saturated colors. Yellow and blue suit almost any other color.
- Repeat color schemes throughout the garden to give a sense of unity.

Bulbs in the Border

Since bulbs are adaptable to any garden design, prairie gardeners may approach border plantings in several ways. Gardeners who want a lavish show of color, and who have plenty of gardening time, can create opulent displays of massed bulbs. Those with a more casual approach, and who prefer a less labor-intensive gardening experience, may be happy to coordinate their bulb border plantings with shrubs and perennials, throwing in a few annuals for good measure.

Formal Bulb Plantings

Most of us have feasted our eyes on expanses of brightly colored tulips in parks or botanical gardens, or in front of grand public buildings. These formal bulb beds are designed to provide a stunning blaze of color for a short time; the bulbs are then removed and replaced with equally flamboyant annual bedding plants.

It is possible to recreate these eye-catching displays in your own garden, achieving the same "wow" factor but on a smaller scale. Indeed, using bulbs as bedding plants, followed by annuals, is a useful technique for making the most of space in a small garden. The beds are colorful from spring until frost, and gardeners have the artistic freedom to change planting patterns from year to year.

A

B

To create perfect partnerships between bulbs and perennials, choose plants with similar bloom times and complementary colors, as illustrated in these attractive combinations: (A) purple veronica (*Veronica spicata)* and coral pink lilies, (B) orange Triumph tulips 'Prinses Irene' and blue grape hyacinth (*Muscari armeniacum*), (C) yellow cypress spurge (*Euphorbia cyparissias* 'Fens Ruby') and red *Tulipa linifolia*, (D) yellow primula (*Primula auricula*) and blue grape hyacinth (*Muscari armeniacum*), (E) yellow narcissus and pink drumstick primula (*Primula denticulata*).

C

D

E

beth Leatherbarrow; (B) Lesley Reynolds; (C) Llyn Strelau; (D) Liesbeth Leatherbarrow; (E) Liesbeth Leatherbarrow

Bulb Design Basics

Garden sizes and styles may vary, but there are some basic principles that apply to all bulb plantings.

- Plant bulbs in large groups. Blocks of color are most effective, so where space and budget allow, plant twelve or more tulips together; plant fifty or more small bulbs in an area; and plant seven of the same variety of lilies, three dahlias or begonias, and twelve of other summer-flowering bulbs.
- Purchase fewer varieties of bulbs to get more of each kind.
- Plant bulbs in drifts or clusters. Avoid planting in a straight line or in a single circle around a tree or shrub.
- Use drifts of two or three colors in each planting area, but do not mix them together.
- Plant early spring bulbs where they enhance other landscape features. Arrange bulb clusters near evergreens, deciduous shrubs with colorful bark, and other features such as benches, birdbaths, or statuary.
- Plant bulbs, particularly early spring bloomers, where they are easily visible from inside the house.
- If bulbs are to be planted far from the house, plant large numbers of a single variety. Massed bulbs stand out from a distance.
- Design bulb plantings to achieve a long bloom season. Different bulbs bloom at different times so if you choose carefully it's possible to enjoy their flowers from spring to fall.
- Combine bulbs with groundcovers, perennials, annuals, trees, and shrubs.
- Plant bulbs closely together for protection from the elements.
- Label bulb plantings to avoid inadvertently slicing through dormant bulbs when you are digging. Either insert markers in the ground or create a map of your bulb plantings.

Of course, there are a few drawbacks to this type of bulb planting. The initial cost of purchasing large quantities of bulbs can be high, and they will need to be replaced with a correspondingly large and expensive number of annuals. It is a labor-intensive process, which involves planting the bulbs in the fall, moving them in late spring, and replacing them with annuals. But for the ultimate display of spring bulbs, there's nothing like it!

Choose one striking bulb variety for blanket planting—classic tulips like Darwin or Triumph hybrids work very well—or choose several varieties that bloom at the same time for a more complex design. Three varieties of different heights work well, but avoid using too many types or colors of bulbs or their impact will be diminished. Since the planting scheme will look its best if all bulbs grow evenly, choose good-quality bulbs of uniform size and ensure that the entire bed has the same soil and light conditions.

After the bulbs have finished flowering, dig them up and replant them in an out-of-the-way corner until the foliage matures. They may then be lifted and stored in a cool, dry place until fall planting time. If you choose early-blooming bulbs for your mass planting, the foliage fades reasonably early in the season and it may be possible to tuck annuals between the bulbs. Alternatively, sow fast-growing annual seeds, such as larkspur, calendula, poppies, and candytuft early in the season to put on a colorful show once the bulbs have faded.

Tender summer bulbs such as gladiolas or dahlias may also be mass planted in the garden, but it is best to pot these up indoors in spring to give them an early start. Bear in mind, however, that they will not give you the summer-long color provided by annuals, and you may wish to slip them between annuals and perennials. Alternatively, limit these bulbs to containers to be brought front and center while in their full glory, and retired once blooms have faded.

Mixed Borders

An informal style involving interplanting bulbs with annuals, perennials, and shrubs suits the casual nature of most prairie gardens, and offers gardeners the opportunity to integrate bulbs with plants of varying sizes, colors, and textures. Even if your borders are crammed with perennials and shrubs, it's easy to tuck bulbs around and between them. Remember that these bulbs will be at their floral peak at a time when perennials are newly emerging and deciduous shrubs are leafless. As perennials reach their full size and shrubs leaf out, the lush early summer growth will soon hide messy dying bulb foliage.

Spring Border Design

The first signs of spring in the mixed border are hardy small bulbs miraculously thrusting their tiny blooms above the mulch and snow. These tough little customers have few floral companions save each other in late March or early April, as they emerge even before the most precocious perennials. You can welcome spring by planting them in generous clusters to truly enjoy the color they'll add to your brown border.

In the absence of perennials in the border, look to shrubs to provide a colorful backdrop to early spring bulbs. The whites, yellows, and blues of snowdrops, crocuses, Siberian and striped squill, and reticulated irises are enhanced by the green or blue-green foliage of low-growing junipers and dwarf varieties of pine or spruce. Red- or yellow-twigged dogwoods and potentillas are striking set amidst a pool of blue Siberian squill.

Keep in mind that the blooming time of spring bulbs largely depends upon where you locate them in your garden. In sunny, open locations, reticulated irises, crocuses, and squill may start blooming as early as the end of March, while in colder, north-facing areas, they may bloom up to a month later.

Once the early spring bulbs have finished blooming, they are succeeded by mid-spring favorites such as narcissus, early tulips, and muscari. Although early spring bulbs are usually small, mid- and late-spring bulbs come in a variety of sizes and bloom heights. At planting time, remember to situate shorter bulbs in front of taller ones. In addition, tall early-blooming narcissus are best placed behind later-blooming tulips so that the view of the tulips won't be spoiled by withering narcissus foliage.

Bulbs that bloom in mid-spring are soon joined by the first perennials of the season. This opens up possibilities for enchanting plant

For informal plantings, bulbs growing in drifts create a more natural and pleasing effect than those regimented in straight lines. *Lesley Reynolds*

Planted en masse for big impact, fringed tulips in a rainbow of pastel shades proclaim the arrival of spring in this prairie botanical garden. *Lesley Reynolds*

Glowing 'Temple of Beauty' tulips, planted four rows deep, create an impressive small scale, formal border. *Liesbeth Leatherbarrow*

Bulbs such as alliums and lilies make flattering companions for large garden statuary. *Lesley Reynolds*

Alliums (*Allium aflatunense* 'Purple Sensation') and tulips combine with magenta fern-leaf peony (*Paeonia tenuifolia*), a blue creeping veronica (*Veronica whitleyi*), and pale pink cranesbill (*Geranium cinereum* 'Ballerina') in a harmonious late-spring, mixed border.
Liesbeth Leatherbarrow

Late to emerge in spring, hostas time their appearance perfectly to hide unsightly maturing bulb foliage. *Ken Girard*

Perennials to Hide Dying Spring Bulb Foliage

The only drawback to planting plenty of spring-flowering bulbs is the unsightly ripening foliage that can persist well into summer. The best solution is to plant perennials with abundant low-growing foliage that will fill in the border by early summer and disguise the dying leaves.

Alchemilla mollis (lady's mantle)
Artemisia absinthium,
  A. ludoviciana, A. schmidtiana,
  A. stelleriana, A. versicolor
  (artemisia)
Astilbe x *arendsii, A. chinensis,*
  A. japonica, A. simplicifolia,
  A. thunbergii, and hybrids
  (false spirea)
Athyrium filix-femina (lady fern)
Geranium endressii,
  G. macrorrhizum, G. x
  magnificum, G. phaeum,
  G. sylvaticum, and hybrids
  (cranesbill)
Heliopsis helianthoides
  (false sunflower)
Hemerocallis fulva,
  H. lilioasphodelus, and hybrids
  (daylily)
Heuchera americana,
  H. x *brizoides, H. cylindrica,*
  H. micrantha, H. sanguinea
  (coral bells)
Hosta fortunei, H. plantaginea,
  H. sieboldiana, and hybrids
  (plantain lily)
Hydrangea arborescens 'Annabelle',
  H. paniculata 'Grandiflora'
  (Pee Gee) (hydrangea)
Lysimachia punctata (yellow
  loosestrife)
Nepeta x *faassenii, N. cataria,*
  N. racemosa, N. sibirica (catmint)
Pulmonaria angustifolia,
  P. longifolia, P. officinalis
  (lungwort)
Tiarella cordifolia, T. wheryii
  (foamflower)

combinations that make the most of the contrast between fleshy, spiky bulb foliage and the softer textures and varying forms of the leaves of newly emerging perennials such as prairie crocuses, ferns, primulas, leopard's bane, peonies, and columbines. If there's room, tuck a few cheerful pansies amidst the tulips and daffodils. Unlike other annuals, they are tough enough to withstand the vagaries of a prairie spring.

Early-flowering shrubs such as forsythia and double flowering plum are fine companions for tulips and narcissus, and what could be prettier than pink or white tulips under a rosybloom crabapple or apple tree in full bloom? By late spring the lilacs are magnificent and look splendid with late tulips and dwarf bearded irises.

Summer Border Design

Many of the loveliest plants adorning prairie gardens each summer grow from bulbs, corms, tubers, rhizomes, and tuberous roots. Hardy lilies and alliums, and tender dahlias, gladiolas, and begonias all fall into this category, as do a host of lesser-used but amazingly beautiful tender summer-flowering bulbs.

Since many summer-flowering bulbs have rigid, straight stems, interplant them with more graceful perennials, annuals, or shrubs. In addition, the stems and maturing leaves of some summer-flowering bulbs, especially lilies, are unattractive after blooming and are best camouflaged by bushy companions. Grouping bulbs amidst perennials as focal points to punctuate a border is effective, particularly in a cottage-style garden.

Summer bulbs often have a tropical extravagance of form and color, and benefit from association with more subtle or delicate plants, rather than similarly flamboyant perennials. Ornamental grasses, Siberian iris, and gray-leaved artemisias are all flattering companions. Some summer bulbs, such as lilies, dahlias, or gladiolas, have a myriad of cultivars and colors, so choose soft shades of these plants if you wish to pair them with boldly colored perennials or annuals.

Fall Border Design

The guidelines to using bulbs in the fall border are simple, since hardy fall bulbs are few in number. Only crocus and *Colchicum* are completely reliable choices for prairie gardens, but if planted in significant numbers, they can be a vital component of the fall landscape. Combine these small bulbs with evergreen shrubs, late-blooming perennials, and plants with interesting or colorful fall foliage, berries, or seed heads. *Colchicum*, which sends up large, rather unattractive leaves in spring, is particularly compatible with groundcovers. Creeping phlox, sedums, creeping veronicas, or thyme—all early bloomers—will disguise the foliage until it dies back and later provide a lovely green backdrop for the fall blossoms.

Other fine partners for fall bulbs are asters, hardy mums, ornamental grasses, and hydrangeas. The two best hydrangeas for the prairies, *Hydrangea arborescens* 'Annabelle' and *H. paniculata* 'Grandiflora' (Pee Gee), both bear huge clusters of white blossoms in late summer and fall.

The Naturalized Bulb Garden

The term "naturalizing" refers to the informal style of planting hardy bulbs in places where they thrive, increase, and look like they just happened there naturally. Naturalizing involves planting bulbs in irregular drifts or random patterns, and in association with compatible companions. The true naturalized garden should require little maintenance, and is not suited to gardeners who are slaves to neatness.

For many gardeners, naturalized bulbs conjure up visions of shady English woodlands carpeted with bluebells and

---

Bulbs with Groundcovers

In addition to providing an attractive backdrop for bulb blossoms, there are several other benefits to combining perennial groundcovers with bulbs. Groundcovers act as a mulch for spring-flowering bulbs, protecting them from winter extremes and early spring thawing and freezing. Spring flowers surrounded by groundcovers won't be splashed by mud, and maturing bulb foliage will be less conspicuous. Groundcovers also help to keep moisture in the ground for summer-flowering bulbs. Try these groundcovers as bulb companions.

Ajuga genevensis, A. pyramidalis, A. reptans (bugleweed)
Arabis caucasica, A. ferdinandi-coburgi (rock cress)
Aubrieta deltoidea (false rock cress)
Campanula portenschlagiana, C. poscharskyana (bellflower)
Cerastium tomentosum (snow-in-summer)
Cornus canadensis (bunchberry)
Galium odoratum (sweet woodruff)
Geranium macrorrhizum, G. sanguineum prostratum (cranesbill)
Iberis saxatilis, I. sempervirens (candytuft)
Lamium galeobdolon, L. maculatum (dead nettle)
Lysimachia nummularia (creeping Jenny)
Omphalodes verna (blue-eyed Mary)
Phlox divaricata, P. stolonifera, P. subulata (phlox)
Potentilla nepalensis, P. tridentata (cinquefoil)
Pulmonaria angustifolia, P. longifolia, P. officinalis (lungwort)
Sedum acre, S. x 'Bertram Anderson', *S. kamtschatiacum, S. sieboldii, S. spurium, S. x* 'Vera Jameson' (stonecrop)
Stachys byzantina (lambs' ears)
Thymus pseudolanuginosus, T. serpyllum (thyme)
Veronica gentianoides, V. pectinata, V. prostrata (speedwell)
Vinca minor (periwinkle)

Garden Plan
(see photo p. 21)

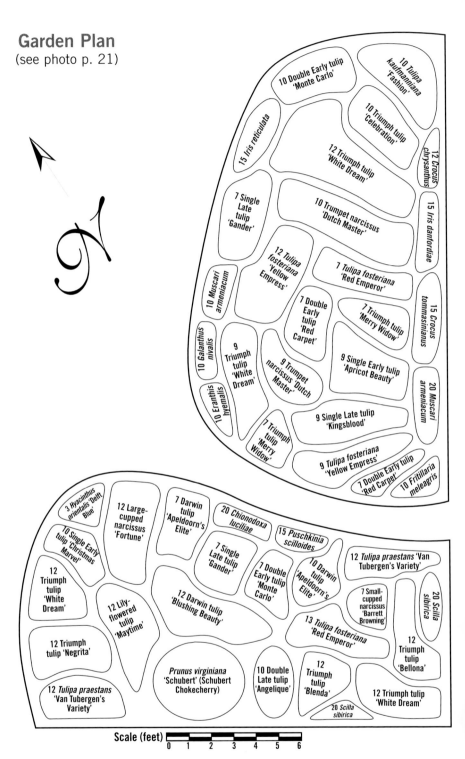

10 Double Early tulip 'Monte Carlo'

10 Tulipa kaufmanniana 'Fashion'

15 Iris reticulata

10 Triumph tulip 'Celebration'

12 Crocus chrysanthus

12 Triumph tulip 'White Dream'

7 Single Late tulip 'Gander'

10 Trumpet narcissus 'Dutch Master'

15 Iris danfordiae

12 Tulipa fosteriana 'Yellow Empress'

7 Tulipa fosteriana 'Red Emperor'

10 Muscari armeniacum

10 Galanthus nivalis

7 Double Early tulip 'Red Carpet'

7 Triumph tulip 'Merry Widow'

15 Crocus tommasinianus

9 Triumph tulip 'White Dream'

9 Trumpet narcissus 'Dutch Master'

9 Single Early tulip 'Apricot Beauty'

20 Muscari armeniacum

10 Eranthis hyemalis

7 Triumph tulip 'Merry Widow'

9 Single Late tulip 'Kingsblood'

9 Tulipa fosteriana 'Yellow Empress'

7 Double Early tulip 'Red Carpet'

10 Fritillaria meleagris

3 Hyacinthus orientalis 'Delft Blue'

12 Large-cupped narcissus 'Fortune'

7 Darwin tulip 'Apeldoorn's Elite'

20 Chionodoxa luciliae

15 Puschkinia scilloides

10 Single Early tulip 'Christmas Marvel'

7 Single Late tulip 'Gander'

7 Double Early tulip 'Monte Carlo'

10 Darwin tulip 'Apeldoorn's Elite'

12 Tulipa praestans 'Van Tubergen's Variety'

12 Triumph tulip 'White Dream'

12 Lily-flowered tulip 'Maytime'

12 Darwin tulip 'Blushing Beauty'

7 Small-cupped narcissus 'Barrett Browning'

20 Scilla sibirica

13 Tulipa fosteriana 'Red Emperor'

12 Triumph tulip 'Negrita'

12 Triumph tulip 'Bellona'

Prunus virginiana 'Schubert' (Schubert Chokecherry)

10 Double Late tulip 'Angelique'

12 Triumph tulip 'Blenda'

12 Tulipa praestans 'Van Tubergen's Variety'

20 Scilla sibirica

12 Triumph tulip 'White Dream'

Scale (feet)
0 1 2 3 4 5 6

This delightful informal bulb border includes a carefully chosen array of bulbs that provide a spectacular show from early to late spring.

lily-of-the-valley or grassy meadows brightened by sunny drifts of daffodils or summer lilies. Prairie gardeners who live on acreages or farms, or who are blessed with especially large town or city lots, may indeed be lucky enough to have woods and meadows where these images of naturalized bulbs can come true. Fortunately, others can settle for nature on a smaller scale by casting a few bulbs beneath a lovely shade tree or creating a meadow in miniature in a lawn or amidst a patch of native or ornamental grasses.

The Naturalized Woodland

Before you begin naturalizing bulbs in a woodland garden, or even in a "cameo" woodland consisting of an area shaded by a tree or two, consider the characteristics of natural woodlands. Woodland bulbs prefer the organically rich soil that typifies the forest floor. They grow vigorously in the spring, before deciduous trees have leafed out, and when sunlight and moisture are most plentiful. Many produce flowers in spring or early summer. Planting under evergreens is not

Hepatica is one of the few perennials that flowers at the same time as Siberian squill (*Scilla sibirica*) and other small, early-blooming bulbs. *Liesbeth Leatherbarrow*

A lavish display of spring-flowering bulbs takes center stage while perennials prepare themselves for a later entrance to the gardening scene (see Garden Plan, p. 20). *Lesley Reynolds*

Bulbs for the Woodland Shade Garden

Allium moly (golden garlic)
Anemone canadensis, A. nemerosa (windflower)
Arisaema (Jack-in-the-pulpit)
Begonia (tuberous begonia)
Chionodoxa (glory-of-the-snow)
Convallaria (lily-of-the-valley)
Corydalis (tuberous corydalis)
Eranthis (winter aconite)
Erythronium (dog's-tooth violet)
Fritillaria meleagris, F. pallidiflora (fritillary)
Galanthus (snowdrop)
Hyacinthoides (bluebell)
Hyacinthus (hyacinth)
Iris (bulbous iris)
Leucojum (snowflake)
Lilium martagon (Turk's cap lily)
Muscari (grape hyacinth)
Narcissus (daffodil)
Nectaroscordum (nectaroscordum)
Puschkinia (striped squill)
Sanguinaria (bloodroot)
Scilla (squill)
Trillium (wakerobin)

advised as these trees allow little light or moisture to reach the forest floor.

Improve the soil in your woodland garden by digging in plenty of compost, peat moss, or well-rotted manure. Group bulbs near pathways at the base of trees, or if you have a large area to work with, plant them in irregular drifts. In the autumn, allow fallen leaves to remain on the ground to protect bulbs and other perennials, nourish the soil, and create a more natural appearance. If plenty of organic material is present, it is not necessary to fertilize naturalized bulbs.

Choose one favorite bulb to predominate in the garden, using a few others as accents in occasional clumps at the base of trees. Most familiar early-flowering bulbs will receive enough spring sunlight to thrive under deciduous trees, and there are many tuberous and rhizomatous woodland natives with a charming variety of flower and foliage shapes, textures, and colors. The intriguing shape of Jack-in-the-pulpit and the delicate flowers of bloodroot, trillium, and dog's-tooth violet will all help to establish a pleasing woodsy atmosphere. Dainty early-blooming perennials, such as hepatica, mertensia, columbines, fernleaf bleeding heart, and violets, will only enhance the bulb display.

The summer woodland garden is the perfect spot for lovely martagon lilies, which thrive in dappled shade. *Allium moly* (golden garlic or lily leek) has yellow flowers and will also do well in light or dappled shade. However, since few other summer-blooming bulbous plants are hardy enough to naturalize on the prairies, it is important to fill your forest with tough shade-loving perennials and groundcovers for summer and autumn interest. For the most pleasing and natural effect, choose native plants or similar cultivated cousins. Ferns, Solomon's seal, spiderwort, and Jacob's ladder are all worthy choices. For groundcovers, select sweet woodruff, lily-of-the-valley, bunchberry, or pulmonaria.

Bulbs and Grasses

Bulbs and grass are natural partners. Many bulbs grow wild in grasslands, taking advantage of the growth cycle of the grass. In spring, while grasses are low and moisture levels relatively high, bulbs produce leaves and flowers. After the bulbs have finished blooming, the grass grows taller, sheltering them from extreme heat as they become dormant. Whether you choose to plant daffodils amidst native grasses in a prairie meadow, or tuck a stream of crocuses in a lawn, the combination is charming.

The Naturalized Bulb Meadow

Gardeners concerned with water conservation can plant a bulb meadow using drought-tolerant, low-maintenance grasses. If your garden is in a rural prairie setting, you may need only to tuck a few bulbs in with existing grasses.

Drought-tolerant grasses are usually clump forming, although newer cultivars are being bred with less of this characteristic. They generally will not give the green, carpeting effect of a conventional lawn, which is usually composed of sod-forming Kentucky bluegrass blended with up to 60 percent creeping red fescue, or Chewing's fescue. Clump-forming grasses have a bristly texture not conducive to barefoot romps and are intolerant of high traffic, as they do not spread by rhizomes.

Bulbs for Grasses

Allium caeruleum, A. cernuum, A. flavum, A. moly, A. oreophilum (ornamental onion)
Camassia (camass)
Fritillaria meleagris, F. pallidiflora, F. pudica (fritillary)
Liatris (gayfeather)
Lilium (lily)
Narcissus (daffodil)
Nectaroscordum (nectaroscordum)
Triteleia (triteleia)
Tulipa tarda, T. turkestanica, T. linifolia (species tulips)

Bulbs for Lawns

Bulbocodium (spring meadow saffron)
Chionodoxa (glory-of-the-snow)
Crocus (crocus)
Galanthus (snowdrop)
Iris (bulbous iris)
Narcissus (early dwarf daffodil)
Puschkinia (striped squill)
Scilla (squill)

However, these grasses are good choices for areas slightly off the beaten track that will be viewed but not walked upon regularly. They require very little water, fertilizer, or herbicide; they also require little mowing, a decided advantage that allows bulb foliage to ripen naturally.

Suitable grasses include hard and sheep fescues (*Festuca ovina* var. *duriuscula, F. ovina*), Canada bluegrass (*Poa compressa*), crested and streambank wheatgrasses (*Agropyron cristatum* [syn. *A. pectiniforme*], *A. riparium*), and Russian wild ryegrass (*Elymus junceus*). Suitable native grasses include northern and western wheatgrasses (*Agropyron dasystachyum, A. smithii*), blue grama (*Bouteloua gracilis*), needle and thread grass (*Stipa comata*), tufted hair grass (*Deschampsia caespitosa*), big bluestem (*Andropogon gerardi*), and little bluestem (*Schizachyrium scoparius*). Avoid planting native grasses in competition with more invasive non-native species.

Ornamental species such as purple moor grass (*Molinia caerulea*), variegated bulbous oat grass (*Arrhenatherum elatius* var. *bulbosum* 'Variegatum'), and blue oat grass (*Helictotrichon sempervirens*) may be grouped with bulbs for a similar effect in miniature. Remember that some grasses, for instance, ribbon grass (*Phalaris arundinacea*), are extremely invasive, a particular problem in small gardens, and should be contained in pots sunk into the ground with the rim at least 5 cm (2 in.) above soil level.

Dotted blazing star (*Liatris punctata*) is at home with other prairie natives such as the prairie coneflower (*Ratibida columnifera*) in a grassy meadow garden. *Lesley Reynolds*

Before planting an area with grasses and bulbs, prepare the soil well. Remove all weeds, then dig in good topsoil and organic material as required to improve soil condition. Late summer is an ideal time to sow grasses as well as plant bulbs. Because these grasses are taller than conventional lawn grasses—many will reach 30 cm (12 in.) or more if unmowed—this is the place for daffodils, fritillaria, lilies, liatris, and alliums.

Grasses may be mown once bulb foliage has ripened. The time will vary depending on which varieties of bulbs are planted.

Bulbs in the Lawn

Many small bulbs look delightful naturalized in a lawn. The trick is to choose hardy, early spring-flowering bulbs that will have completed blooming and ripening foliage (about eight weeks) before the lawn needs to be mowed. Some bulbs, such as Siberian and striped squill, will also self-seed if seeds are allowed to ripen. Gardeners who try this may need to tolerate a less than neat and trim lawn until June or, alternatively, take the time to hand-clip the grass around clumps of bulb foliage.

Choose a sunny area of lawn where bulbs will begin their growth cycle in early spring. Recommended bulbs are hardy enough to tolerate the below-freezing overnight temperatures common to a prairie spring.

Naturalized Siberian squill (*Scilla sibirica*), glory-of-the-snow (*Chionodoxa luciliae*), and striped squill (*Puschkinia scilloides*) carpet the floor of a woodland garden in early spring. *Liesbeth Leatherbarrow*

Plant bulbs in clumps or in ribbons across the lawn. To plant groups of small bulbs, cut out the turf in the planting areas, loosen the exposed soil, and amend it with compost. Refill the hole to the desired planting depth for the bulbs you have chosen. Place the bulbs in the hole, and cover them with the soil-compost mix. Score the bottom of the turf with a hand garden fork, then re-lay the turf, press it down, and water the area. Alternatively, dig individual holes for each small bulb with a bulb planter, digging slightly deeper than the desired depth, and adding a little soil-compost mix to each hole before planting the bulb.

Flowers may be removed as bulbs fade. The bulbs will benefit from lawn fertilizer, but try to avoid herbicides, as they may damage bulbs.

Lilies and alliums are stars of the mid-summer border. *Liesbeth Leatherbarrow*

Rock Gardens

Many bulbs that evolved in alpine climates find the rock garden habitat exactly to their liking. By providing excellent drainage, rock gardens circumvent the problem of heavy clay soil, and the rocks absorb heat and shelter plants. In addition, small alpine perennials, many of which bloom early, are delightful companions for spring-flowering bulbs. Rock gardens are suitable for any size of garden; they can be impressive structures or scaled-down versions ideal for a collection of tiny alpines. And, since these gardens are raised above soil level, they provide a welcome variation in height, and allow easy viewing of plants.

The diminutive stature and exquisite beauty of *Tulipa pulchella* 'Persian Pearl', growing beside yellow *Vitaliana primuliflora*, make it a perfect candidate for rock gardens. *Liesbeth Leatherbarrow*

Rock gardens should be constructed in a sunny location. If you have an existing slope, so much the better—you don't have to mow a rock garden. For a natural appearance, choose only one type of rock, and layer it like a natural outcrop, rather than dotting odd stones here and there. Prepare a gritty soil mix by using a mixture of one-third rock grit, one-third playbox sand, and one-third organic material, such as compost or peat moss. Alternatively, special alpine mixes are available at some landscape supply companies. Mulch with a 2.5-cm (1-in.) layer of rock chips or grit.

The best bulbs for rock gardens are small, to complement low-growing alpine perennials. If your garden resembles the Rockies, you may be able to plant taller species, but remember that large dying bulb leaves may overwhelm small perennials, so place them accordingly.

Container Gardens

When prairie gardeners think of pots on patios, visions of geraniums rather than gladiolas are more likely to dance through their heads. However, many bulbs make a spectacular show in containers, particularly the exotic summer-flowering bulbs that are available in garden centers each spring.

Whether you choose to cultivate annuals, perennials, vegetables, or bulbs, container gardening offers many advantages. Containers can transform a small square of patio into a lush green retreat. They are convenient, easy to maintain, and usually need no weeding. Their portability makes it easier to cope with the unpredictability of prairie weather, since pots may be grouped in a sheltered area, covered, or even moved indoors when threatened by frost, hail, thunderstorms, or strong winds. Portability is also an asset if you wish to put color where perennials have finished blooming for the season. And once the bulbs have finished blooming, the pots can be whisked away to where the foliage can ripen in privacy.

Choose formal or informal containers to suit your garden style. Terracotta, ceramic, wood, plastic, fibreglass, concrete, and metal pots are all perfectly suitable for growing bulbs, provided they have drainage holes. Terracotta pots dry out the fastest, so are ideal for species that prefer dry conditions after blooming. Since ceramic pots are often patterned, you need to coordinate flower colors with the pot design. As with terracotta, wooden containers have an earthy feel that suits all kinds of plants, except the most stiff and formal plantings. Shallow, wide containers show off small- to medium-sized bulbs to great advantage, but make sure they are large enough—when the bulb is planted at its required depth, there should be the same amount of soil below it as above. Some summer-flowering bulbs grow very tall, so their containers must be in proportion to the height of the bulbs.

Spring Bulbs in Containers

On the prairies, growing spring-flowering bulbs in containers is a challenge. Bulbs planted in above-ground pots or planters will not withstand the extreme temperatures of a prairie winter, to say nothing of the freeze-thaw cycles particularly common throughout the Chinook Zone.

The key to success with container-grown spring bulbs is to keep them insulated over the winter months. First, plant the bulbs to their required depth in plastic pots—clay may shatter with the cold. Plant bulbs close together, but not touching, and water them well. Pots may then be sunk into a plunge bed, that is, an area filled with peat moss or sand that will insulate the bulbs from repeated freezing and thawing, but will not freeze solid. This allows the pots to be easily exhumed in the spring.

Fragrant Bulbs

Allium flavum, A. tuberosum (ornamental onion)
Babiana (baboon flower)
Convallaria (lily-of-the-valley)
Crinum (crinum lily)
Freesia (freesia)
Galanthus (snowdrop)
Gladiolus callianthus (peacock orchid)
Hyacinthoides non-scripta (English bluebell)
Hyacinthus (hyacinth)
Hymenocallis (spider lily)
Iris reticulata (bulbous iris)
Leucojum (snowflake)
Lilium (lily), 'Starburst Sensation', 'Northern Carillon', 'Northern Sensation', 'Northern Beauty'
Narcissus (daffodil), 'Carlton', 'Cheerfulness', 'Sir Winston Churchill', 'Yellow Cheerfulness', as well as Triandrus, Jonquilla, and Tazetta cultivars, *N. poeticus* var. *recurvus*, and Poeticus cultivars
Tulipa (tulip), 'Abba', 'Ad Rem', 'Allegretto', 'Angelique', 'Apricot Beauty', 'Ballerina', 'Christmas Dream', 'Couleur Cardinal', 'Daydream', 'Electra', 'Generaal de Wet', 'Monte Carlo', 'Mr. Van der Hoef', 'Prinses Irene', 'Salmon Pearl', 'Schoonoord', 'White Emperor', and species *T. kolpakowskiana, T. tarda*

Lastly, apply a thick layer of mulch over the pots. Alternatively, fill a cold-frame with dry peat moss, shredded leaves, or sand, and sink the pots into it, again covering the pots with mulch. In spring, when temperatures begin to warm, gradually remove the mulch; when shoots begin to show, you can dig up the pots and put them on display. Arrange several small pots of flowering bulbs in a large decorative container filled with peat moss. As flowers finish blooming, you can remove these pots and replace them with others as they come into bloom. This technique also works to keep summer bulb displays looking fresh.

Container-grown spring bulbs should be stored in a cool place once the foliage has ripened. As they are unlikely to perform well for two seasons in pots, plant them in the garden in the fall and begin the process with new bulbs.

Old pheasant's eye narcissus (*Narcissus poeticus* var. *recurvus*) is not only lovely to look at but is also a fragrant addition to the late-spring border. *Liesbeth Leatherbarrow*

Lilies planted in widely spaced rows allow for easy mechanical cultivation between the rows in this prairie cutting garden. *Liesbeth Leatherbarrow*

Tender peacock orchids (*Gladiolus callianthus*) provide elegant beauty and fragrance in containers in late summer and early fall. *Lesley Reynolds*

Proper conditioning will extend the vase life of cut flowers, such as these stems of the tender Peruvian lily (*Alstroemeria*). *Lesley Reynolds*

29

Another option is to construct square or rectangular wooden boxes lined with styrofoam to overwinter spring bulbs and lilies. The planters should be at least 60 cm (24 in.) deep and wide. Before filling the boxes, move them to where the bulbs will be on display in the spring (a sheltered area is best), and construct a styrofoam-lined lid to put on the planted boxes once the soil has frozen. Concrete planters are also fairly well insulated and, if they are large enough and are covered for the winter, can also be used for spring bulbs.

Once the bulbs have finished blooming, dig them up and replant them in your garden, either permanently or just until the foliage matures, when they may be lifted and stored until fall. Fill the vacated planters with annuals to provide color all summer long.

Summer Bulbs in Containers

Pots of summer-flowering bulbs lend an exotic air to any garden. Choose several species with different bloom times to enjoy a succession of flowers until fall. Many summer bulbs are deliciously fragrant; as they come into bloom, move them near your favorite seating area in the garden to better enjoy their delightful perfumes.

To get an early start, plant summer-flowering bulbs indoors in a sterile potting mix about six weeks before the last expected frost date (since a few bulbs need to be planted earlier, consult individual plant descriptions). Alternatively, bulbs may be planted directly into containers outdoors, one to two weeks before the last expected frost date; however, these bulbs will bloom much later than those started indoors. Plant only one type of bulb per container or mix bulbs with annuals. Planting several varieties with different bloom times in one pot will result in dying foliage in the same pot with newly blooming bulbs. Move containers of bulbs started indoors into the garden when the risk of frost has passed, but keep them in a warm location—some tropical bulbs are very sensitive to cool temperatures. Containers of spent bulbs can be moved to an out-of-the-way corner for the foliage to ripen, and the bulbs may then be lifted and stored.

Cutting Gardens

When little else is blooming, bulb gardens supply many varieties of splendid flowers to cut for indoor floral arrangements. But since many gardeners treasure their outdoor floral displays too much to cut flowers from them, some choose to set aside space for a cutting garden. One area can serve double duty for both spring- and summer-flowering bulbs if spring bulbs are lifted and heeled in elsewhere to ripen.

Choose a sunny area with fertile, well-drained soil. For ease of cutting, plant the bulbs in rows three or four bulbs deep, inserting stakes for tall flowers such as gladiolas or dahlias at the time of planting to avoid inadvertently damaging bulbs at a later date. Mulch the planting area to protect spring bulbs from coming up prematurely, to preserve soil moisture, and to keep the flowers clean. Fertilize the plants regularly once the buds begin to open and until the foliage begins to die back. Once the leaves are brown, the bulbs may be lifted and stored for the following year. If you don't have space for a cutting garden, try planting extra bulbs in large groups in the border and thin out these clusters when you need blooms for flower arrangements.

When it is time to harvest flowers, choose buds that have just started to open; immature buds may not open properly. Avoid a clearcut look by cutting flowers from the middle or back of the rows or by cutting alternate flowers.

Best Bulbs for Cutting

Agapanthus (lily-of-the-Nile)
Alstroemeria (Peruvian lily)
Anemone coronaria (windflower)
Babiana (baboon flower)
Camassia (camass)
Canna (canna)
Crinum (crinum lily)
Crocosmia (montbretia)
Dahlia (dahlia)
Eremurus (foxtail lily)
Eucomis (pineapple flower)
Freesia (freesia)
Gladiolus (gladiola)
Hymenocallis (spider lily)
Iris (iris)
Liatris (gayfeather)
Lilium (lily)
Narcissus (daffodil)
Nerine (Guernsey lily)
Ornithogalum (star-of-Bethlehem)
Sparaxis (harlequin flower)
Triteleia (triteleia)
Tritonia (flame freesia)
Tulipa (tulip)
Watsonia (bugle lily)
Zantedeschia (calla lily)

Miniature arrangements:
Chionodoxa (glory-of-the-snow)
Convallaria (lily-of-the-valley)
Galanthus (snowdrop)
Leucojum (snowflake)
Muscari (grape hyacinth)
Puschkinia (striped squill)
Scilla (squill)

Conditioning Cut Flowers

The best time to harvest flowers is early in the morning when they are at their freshest. You require a sharp knife to cut the flowers and a bucket of tepid water. Avoid using scissors as they crush the stems. When you cut the blossoms, leave as much foliage on the plants as possible to replenish the bulb's energy stores.

Immediately place the cut flowers into the bucket of water, entirely immersing the stems. This is particularly helpful in keeping tulip stems straight. Leave the flowers in a cool room away from direct sunlight for several hours to acclimatize them to warmer indoor temperatures. The flowers can then be arranged in a container with fresh water and a cut-flower food. Remove leaves below the water line to prevent bacterial growth in the water and recut the stems on a slant. To keep flowers fresh, place them out of direct sunlight. Replace the water and cut off a little of the stems every second day.

Because cut narcissus exude a poisonous sap that will shorten the life of other cut flowers, either arrange them on their own or condition them separately before putting them in a vase with other flowers. To condition them, leave them standing in a bucket of cold water for several hours. It is then safe to put them with other flowers.

Buying Bulbs

N othing compares to the delicious sense of anticipation that accompanies the ritual of buying bulbs for the garden—be it a late-summer expedition to the local garden center or the time spent poring over specialty catalogues and placing an order. Indeed, imagining the display of spring color to come is almost as pleasurable as admiring their charm and beauty right in your own spring garden.

The decision to buy bulbs in person at a local garden center or sight unseen via mail-order catalogue usually depends on a gardener's needs and expectations. There are definite advantages to selecting bulbs directly from display bins in garden centers: they can be handpicked for health, uniform size, and color (if accidental mixing has not taken place in the bins). However, the variety of bulbs available at garden centers is usually limited to popular species and cultivars that have proven successful in the region served by the garden center. This is good for beginning bulb enthusiasts as it takes the guesswork out of choosing and, barring unforeseen circumstances, ensures a certain measure of success.

Inviting displays of spring-flowering bulbs tempt eager gardeners in late summer and early fall. *Lesley Reynolds*

For more adventuresome or experienced gardeners, mail-order catalogues are often the way to go. They offer a wide selection of bulb species and cultivars, enough to satisfy the needs of even the most avid bulb collector. The disadvantage is that those who make mail-order purchases must rely on the supplier to send healthy bulbs of uniform size and the desired cultivar. Although this entails taking risks, these can be minimized by ordering from reputable establishments.

You Get What You Pay For!

When it comes to buying bulbs, remember that you get what you pay for—quality bulbs produce quality flowers, which is inevitably reflected in their price. For big impact and top performance in the garden, choose top-sized bulbs. They usually give a considerable bang for the proverbial buck, not only producing larger blossoms but often more of them than average-sized bulbs do. The superior results are well worth the added expense, especially for those parts of the garden where an elaborate display of spring color is intended.

In general, bargain bulbs are sold at a discount because they do not measure up to industry standards, either in size or quality. Usually they are smaller or younger versions of their more expensive counterparts and often take a few years to establish before they produce blossoms. This makes them a good choice for naturalizing in the garden or tucking into corners where an elaborate display is not so important for the first year or two.

If you are willing to take a chance, bins of "mystery" bulbs are a good place to find quality bulbs at discount prices. These usually comprise a mix of leftover bulbs, or those that have lost their labels.

When to Buy Bulbs

Bulbs are available in garden centers and mail-order catalogues either in late summer and fall or in early spring, depending on their hardiness and cultural requirements.

- Buy bare spring- and summer-flowering hardy bulbs such as tulips and daffodils in late summer; plant them outdoors in the fall.
- Buy container-grown spring- and summer-flowering bulbs such as lilies, liatris, and iris in spring and early summer; plant them outdoors in spring and early summer.
- Buy bare summer-flowering tender bulbs such as gladiolas and dahlias in early spring; start them indoors in containers about six weeks (see individual plant descriptions) before the last average frost date, and move them outdoors after all threat of frost has passed. These bulbs may also be planted directly in the garden one to two weeks before the last average frost date.
- Buy bulbs for indoor forcing in late summer or early fall; pre-chill and plant them as desired during the winter.

Buying Bulbs from Garden Centers

Gardeners are well advised to be quick when it comes to buying bulbs from garden centers. The earlier you buy, the greater the variety of available bulbs and the better their quality. Another good reason to buy early is to get bulbs into the ground with plenty of time for them to establish roots before the soil freezes. Daffodils, especially, benefit from early planting on the prairies—no later than September 15 is recommended. However, not all bulb shipments arrive at the same time, so if you have a long and varied wish list, you may need to return to your favorite garden-center haunt a few times to acquire everything on your list.

Ordering Bulbs from Foreign Sources

Canada has very strict regulations for importing bulbs or plants to protect local species from the introduction of devastating new plant pests. As an importer, you are responsible for being familiar with these rules and for informing your foreign supplier about them. Also, be aware that some plants are prohibited entry into Canada and that there is a worldwide ban on importing rare or endangered species.

Several steps must be taken to successfully import bulbs or plants. In addition to obtaining a "Permit to Import" from Agriculture Canada, you must also obtain a phytosanitary certificate from your foreign supplier declaring that the plants/bulbs to be imported are disease and pest free. This requires an inspection to be done by local officials, and the signed certificate must accompany your shipment to the border. At the border, your shipment will be inspected and the phytosanitary certificate checked. A cost is incurred to you, the importer, at each step along the way. If your shipment is given a clean bill of health, Canada Customs will charge you the appropriate duty and GST, and release the shipment. If there are problems, the shipment will be refused entry, or it may be confiscated and destroyed. For more details, get in touch with Agriculture Canada.

There are similar requirements regarding the importation of plant material into the United States. However, regulations vary from state to state and it is your responsibility as the importer to familiarize yourself with the requirements and to see that they are implemented.

At garden centers, bulbs can be bought prepackaged or loose from open bins. You can be most discriminating when you choose your bulbs from bins, although if what you want is only available in the prepackaged form, go for it! Just remember that you're taking a bit of a gamble; it's harder and sometimes impossible to check the bulbs' physical state inside packaging.

Here are some tips for buying bulbs at garden centers.

- Choose plump, firm bulbs that are heavy for their size.
- Choose bulbs that are of comparable size (planted at the same depth, they will bloom at the same time).
- Avoid soft, mushy, moldy bulbs.
- Avoid bulbs with damaged tunics, especially if the fleshy part beneath has also been damaged or has begun to shrivel and dry out.
- Avoid bulbs that have sprouted in the bin.
- Avoid bulbs that have been displayed in a sunny location or too close to a vent, both of which can cause rapid deterioration in bulb quality.
- **Warning:** Bulbs are usually dusted with a fungicide powder, so always wash your hands after handling them.

Buying Bulbs from Mail-order Catalogues

Gardeners love to browse and linger over glossy catalogues in anticipation of placing an order. The full-color photographs are always a temptation and undoubtedly the sole inspiration for many a gardener's purchase. However, it is often the catalogues without illustrations that offer the best choices. With well-written, detailed descriptions, they can be just as helpful and as enticing as their more flamboyant counterparts.

Some mail-order establishments are generalists, simply serving as intermediaries between bulb brokers or specialists and their customers. They offer a decent range of choices from a list of many different bulb types, and sometimes perennials and annuals as well. The freshness of their products is usually the same as that in good retail nurseries and garden centers.

Other mail-order establishments pride themselves in being specialists, growing and developing their own fresh stock and shipping it directly to customers. Specialists usually offer an extensive list of cultivars of a limited number of bulb types, and it is their catalogues that will offer you true adventure in discovering the new, the rare, the unusual, the bizarre, the curious, and the exceptional. Specialty catalogues are

Some bulbs, such as these snowdrops (*Galanthus nivalis*), are endangered in the wild and should only be purchased as "bulbs grown from cultivated stock." *Lesley Reynolds*

also the perfect stomping grounds for gardeners with a hankering for collecting.

Many mail-order catalogues are now available online, a real bonus for computer users. As with ordinary catalogues, some online catalogues are beautifully illustrated whereas others rely on detailed written descriptions to lure customers. Almost all offer the option of placing orders online, which is usually a quick, straightforward procedure that bypasses the need for compiling lengthy lists and filling out forms.

If you are just venturing into the realm of mail-order catalogues, collect recommendations from experienced friends or local horticultural groups for one or two reliable organizations. Alternatively, choose a mail-order company that suits your purposes, make yourself familiar with their guarantee and refund policy, and place a small first-time order to evaluate their bulbs and services. If the company doesn't meet your expectations or honor its guarantee, at least your losses will be minimal.

Some tips for ordering from mail-order catalogues follow.

- Order bulbs early as they are shipped on a "first ordered, first served" basis and supplies are often limited. You might also get a discounted price on top-quality bulbs just by ordering before a specified date.
- If your newly arrived bulbs have sprouted, and you decide not to

Storing Bulbs Before Planting

Whether you purchase bulbs from a local retailer or order them "from away," there is often a delay between arrival day and planting day. Here are a few tips on how to keep your bulbs fresh until you can get them into the ground.

- Keep spring-flowering bulbs cool and dry by storing them in paper bags in a garage or storage shed with good air circulation, or in a refrigerator with the temperature set just above freezing (4° C, 40° F); excessive heat damages the dormant flower bud inside true bulbs and the growth points on corms, tubers, and rhizomes.
- Keep bulbs stored in a refrigerator away from apples and other fruit that produce ethylene while ripening; ethylene gas damages the dormant flower bud inside true bulbs and the growth points on corms, tubers, and rhizomes.
- Do not store bulbs in a freezer; they will turn to mush.
- Keep summer-flowering bulbs warm and dry by storing them indoors at room temperature (20° C, 68° F).

take up the matter with your supplier, plant them straight away at the proper depth and mulch with a thick layer of leaves to keep the soil and bulbs cool, thus preventing further sprouting.

- If you can, specify a shipping time that avoids the need to store bulbs any longer than necessary before getting them into the ground. Otherwise, note their shipping time and plan to be home around the scheduled delivery date, again so the bulbs can be planted pronto!
- If prices for a specific bulb are significantly lower in one catalogue than in another, usually the difference in cost is a function of bulb size—the larger the bulb, the higher the price tag. This difference won't matter in the long run, but it will definitely affect performance in the first year after planting.
- Beware that some catalogues are illustrated with composite photos, designed to include an arbitrary selection of bulb genera and species that don't necessarily bloom at the same time, although the composite may give the impression they do.

5 Planting Bulbs

Many bulbs are surprisingly forgiving of haphazard planting and less-than-ideal soil conditions. However, since they often represent a considerable monetary investment, not to mention the time spent actually getting them into the ground, it's well worth making the effort to plant them properly.

Choose a site with good drainage—gentle slopes or slightly raised beds are ideal. Few bulbs thrive in boggy locations, and many prefer soil on the dry side during summer dormancy. Most bulbs prefer full to part sun, although a spot under a deciduous tree that is sunny in early spring and lightly shaded in summer is perfect for many of them. Avoid planting bulbs under evergreens, as there is certain to be insufficient light or moisture in this environment. Check the specific cultural requirements of each bulb to choose the perfect location.

Ideally, hardy bulbs will stay in place for many years, and the quantity and quality of their blooms, as well as their inclination to spread, will be affected by the quality of the soil. The best soil for all bulbs is a good loam that is moderately fertile, retains water reasonably well, and drains well. In some areas of the prairies, the soil has a high clay content; in other areas, the soil is sandy. Both types will be improved by the addition of plenty of organic material, such as compost, composted manure, or moistened peat moss.

Compost and composted manure improve soil fertility and tilth. Although peat moss adds few nutrients to the soil, it does increase moisture retention, improve tilth, and lower soil pH in areas of high alkalinity. Mix these amendments into the soil to a depth of 30 cm (12 in.) to ensure an abundance of fertile soil beneath the bulbs. Some gardeners find it easiest to excavate soil out of a small section of the planting area onto a tarpaulin or sheet of plastic, mix the amendments into this pile, and then replace the soil, before moving on to the next section and repeating the process. Water the amended bed a few days before planting to allow it to settle. At planting time the soil should be slightly moist but not muddy.

When to Plant

Most of the hardy bulbs grown by prairie gardeners bloom in spring or early summer. They are usually available in garden centers in late August for fall planting. If you are ordering from a catalogue, make sure that the bulbs will arrive by early September.

Ideally, all bulbs should be planted as soon as possible after purchase to give them time to establish strong roots before the ground freezes. However, gardeners, like garden writers, have busy lives, and they also tend to buy more bulbs than can be planted expeditiously. If you can't plant your bulbs promptly store them in paper bags in a cool, dry place with good air circulation (see Chapter 4, p. 38, Storing Bulbs Before Planting). When you do find time to plant, certain bulbs should take priority. Tubers and fritillaries, which have lilylike bulbs without tunics, dry out quickly and should be first in the planting schedule. Plant small bulbs next, as they become desiccated sooner than large bulbs. Daffodils require several weeks of decent weather to grow roots so should be planted no later than mid-September. If planted too late, they may not bloom well during their first year, although they should do well in subsequent years. Tulips are the most forgiving—many a tardy gardener who plants them as the snow flies in early November is rewarded with bloom the following spring.

Tender bulbs for summer bloom are purchased in spring. For an earlier start to the season, pot them up indoors to be moved outside after all risk of frost has passed. The bulbs can also be planted directly into the garden, but only about one to two weeks before the last expected frost, so there is no risk of frost damaging the emerging shoots. Although also available for planting in the fall, lilies are best planted in spring; they can be purchased at garden centers potted up and ready to bloom.

Fall-blooming crocus and *Colchicum* are available in late summer and should be planted immediately after purchase. They bloom in short order, almost instantly rewarding the impatient gardener.

How to Plant

Examine the bulbs before you plant them and wipe off any blue-gray powdery mold that may have formed. Discard any bulbs that are soft or rotten, or dried out. Tubers or tunic-less bulbs, such as lilies and fritillaries, that appear a bit dehydrated may plump up if they are placed in moistened peat moss or between wet paper towels for a few hours. If they don't plump up, discard them.

As a rule, bulbs should be planted in groups, so it is easiest to use a small spade to dig a single trench that will accommodate each group. This ensures that all the bulbs are planted at the proper depth and will come up and bloom at the same time. Where the soil is full of roots, such as around established perennials, trees, and shrubs, it may be necessary to dig individual holes. In this case, dig the hole deeper than necessary and add a layer of amended soil beneath the bulb. The most useful tool for bulb planting is a simple trowel, although commercial bulb planters can be used to dig individual holes. These tools are pushed into the earth and remove a core of soil; however, they may not dig deeply enough for large bulbs.

Refer to the planting-depth chart (p. 42) or to individual bulb descriptions to determine the proper depth and for specific planting tips for each type of bulb you wish to plant. Generally, planting depth is about three times the height of the bulb, measured to the base of the bulb. Place the bulbs in the prepared soil pointed side up and push them down firmly to ensure that the base of the bulb is in close contact with the soil. Fill the trench with soil, and water the area well. If compost or manure has been added to the soil, it should not be necessary to fertilize at this time. Alternatively, mix a slow-release bulb fertilizer (9-9-6) into the soil that is replaced in the planting trench. Fungicides are not usually necessary, but gardeners who have repeatedly experienced problems with rotted bulbs, and who have eliminated poor drainage as the cause, may wish to sprinkle the bulbs with a bulb dust as they are planted.

Once the bulbs are planted, apply a layer of organic mulch, such as shredded leaves or compost, over the planting area. Use only a thin layer (2.5 to 5 cm, 1 to 2 in.) of mulch over tiny bulbs, such as crocus, snowdrops, or striped and Siberian squill, or it will be too difficult for them to push through. A 10-cm (4-in.) layer may be applied over larger bulbs such as tulips or daffodils. Mulch helps retain soil moisture and deters spring-flowering bulbs such as daffodils from coming up prematurely. This is particularly important in the Chinook Zone, where temperatures may soar in mid-winter and insulating snow cover is generally unreliable. Mulching is also a useful practice for summer-flowering bulbs to help retain soil moisture, deter weeds, and supply further organic material to the soil.

Since all traces of spring-flowering bulbs virtually disappear by fall

On the prairies, the general rule is to plant the bottoms of bulbs at a depth equal to three times their height, and space them at intervals of one or two times their width. *Lesley Reynolds*

Bulb Planting Depth Chart for Hardy and Borderline Prairie Bulbs

This chart gives the preferred planting depths of bulbs. Plants that show a wide range of planting depths in the chart, such as *Allium* and *Lilium*, grow from bulbs that come in a range of sizes, depending on the species. Plant smaller bulbs at the shallow end of the range and larger bulbs at the deep end of the range.

Bulb (Botanical Name)	Common Name	<2.5 cm (1 in.)	2.5 cm (1 in.)	5 cm (2 in.)	7.5 cm (3 in.)	10 cm (4 in.)	12.5 cm (5 in.)	15 cm (6 in.)	17.5 cm (7 in.)	20 cm (8 in.)
Allium	ornamental onion			•	•	•	•	•	•	•
Anemone	windflower				•					
Anemonella	rue anemone			•	•					
Arisaema	Jack-in-the-pulpit			•	•					
Bulbocodium	spring meadow saffron				•					
Camassia	camass					•	•			
Chionodoxa	glory-of-the-snow				•					
Colchicum	autumn crocus					•				
Convallaria	lily-of-the-valley		•							
Corydalis	tuberous corydalis			•	•					
Crocus	crocus			•	•					
Eranthis	winter aconite				•					
Eremurus	foxtail lily					•	•	•		
Erythronium	dog's-tooth violet			•	•					
Fritillaria	fritillary						•			
Galanthus	snowdrop			•	•					
Hyacinthoides	bluebell					•				
Hyacinthus	hyacinth							•		
Iris, bearded	bearded iris	•								
Iris, bulbous	bulbous iris				•	•				
Ixiolirion	ixia lily							•		
Leucojum	snowflake			•	•					
Liatris	gayfeather				•					
Lilium	lily					•	•	•	•	•
Muscari	grape hyacinth			•						
Narcissus, hybrids	daffodil, hybrids						•	•	•	•
Narcissus, miniature	daffodil, miniature				•	•				
Nectaroscordum	nectaroscordum					•	•	•		
Ornithogalum	star-of-Bethlehem			•						
Oxalis	wood sorrel			•						
Puschkinia	striped squill				•					
Sanguinaria	bloodroot	•								
Scilla	squill				•	•				
Trillium	wakerobin				•					
Triteleia	triteleia				•	•	•			
Tulipa, hybrids	tulip, hybrids							•	•	
Tulipa, species	tulip, species						•			

bulb-planting time, it is advisable to clearly mark or map where they are planted. It is also important to know the location of late-emerging lilies during spring planting. Accurate labeling not only helps gardeners to avoid damaging subterranean bulbs when digging in apparently vacant areas, but it also allows them to better coordinate colors and bloom times when planting in subsequent years.

6 Caring for Bulbs

In their native habitat, bulbs can fend for themselves; clever evolutionary adaptations allow them to survive whatever circumstances nature sends their way. In prairie gardens, however, both hardy and tender bulbs experience only some of the climatic conditions to which they are accustomed. For this reason and for the obvious esthetic ones, gardeners need to give bulbs a modest amount of tender loving care while they are in their safekeeping.

The list of maintenance tasks for bulbs is a simple one, not much different from the equivalent list for perennials and annuals. It consists of watering, fertilizing, deadheading, mulching, staking, and checking bulbs for pests and disease. By devoting a small amount of time to looking after their basic needs, you will ensure that even the most exotic bulbs put on a fabulous show in the challenging prairie climate.

Watering

With very few exceptions, bulbs have the same water requirements. They need a thorough watering at the time of planting, even and constant moisture levels during root development and active growth, and a moderately dry period during dormancy. Hardy bulbs planted in the fall become dormant during the summer, after the foliage has turned yellow or brown, which is usually several weeks after they have finished blooming. Reduce watering during this period; however, if your bulbs are overplanted with thirsty perennials with a continuous need for water, don't worry. Perfectly happy to stay on the dry side, the bulbs will leave the water for the perennials. Tender bulbs planted in the spring become dormant during the winter, after they have been lifted in the fall for indoor storage. These bulbs require no watering until active growth restarts in the spring, although some may need to be kept in a damp medium during dormancy to prevent shriveling.

Water bulbs deeply so that the water actually reaches their root zone, where water absorption takes place. Watering depth will vary with bulb type, but narcissus, for example, which are usually planted about 15 cm (6 in.) deep, have a root system that extends another 15 cm (6 in.);

clearly, narcissus need to be watered to a minimum depth of 30 cm (12 in.). Also, do your best not to let bulbs dry out during active growth—with insufficient water, thirsty plants may sulk and perform poorly.

Soaker hoses or hand-held watering wands that allow you to steer the water flow directly to the soil surface are probably the best tools for the task, if you have a choice. Unfortunately, prolonged overhead watering, even from falling rain, can result in big blossoms drooping and tender stems flopping. Tulips and crocuses are especially vulnerable to collecting water in their goblet-shaped blossoms, but thanks to nature's wisdom, their blossoms remain closed on cloudy days, so rain isn't a problem for them. However, nature has yet to figure out how to help tulips and crocuses cope with overhead sprinklers on a sunny day.

Fertilizing

Because both tender and hardy bulbs come prepackaged naturally with enough food to sustain them during one growth cycle, they often do quite well without the addition of any fertilizer the first year. However, studies have shown that bulbs perform better with an application of fertilizer at the time of planting. Another key time for fertilizing bulbs occurs after they have finished blooming, when their foliage is ripening and manufacturing their next year's food supply. Established clumps of hardy bulbs also appreciate a nutrient boost when they resume active growth—immediately after the ground has thawed and again in the fall, after summer dormancy but before freeze-up.

One of the best sources for bulb nutrients is good, old-fashioned compost. When used on a regular basis, it contains enough nitrogen (N), phosphorus (P), potassium (K), and trace elements to see most bulbs through many a growing season. Simply work a handful of compost into the soil at the bottom of the planting hole, top dress with compost in spring and again in summer while the foliage is ripening, and your bulbs will, for the most part, be happy.

Many gardeners also like to use bonemeal as part of their bulbs' dietary regime; it's a good source of phosphorus and an important ingredient for root and bulb development. Bonemeal (and other phosphorus-bearing fertilizer) is only really effective, however, when incorporated into the soil surrounding a bulb's root zone. This is because phosphorus does not readily dissolve in water and, therefore, is relatively immobile. Very little, if any, is transported to the root zone from the surface by rain or irrigation. Instead, phosphorus binds to soil particles on contact, only to be released very slowly into its immediate surroundings to a maximum depth of just 2 or 3 cm (0.75 to 1.2 in.). Unfortunately, the active root zone of most bulbs is located much deeper than that, and will only receive small amounts of the phosphorus from a surface application of bonemeal or other fertilizer.

The situation is similar, though not as extreme, for potassium in fertilizers, some of which also becomes insoluble on contact with soil. Of the three major elements required for healthy plants—nitrogen, phosphorus, and potassium—nitrogen is the most water soluble and transportable to deep root zones by rain or irrigation. This makes it the major element that is most usefully applied to the soil surface. Although some potassium does percolate to a bulb's root zone, it and phosphorus are most effective when applied directly in the planting hole.

An interesting corollary to this bit of chemistry is that, because of its inclination to bind itself to soil particles, phosphorus concentration quickly builds in soils, and after many years of fertilization, further addition of phosphorus in fertilizers is likely not necessary.

In truth, there are almost as many recommendations for a good manufactured bulb fertilizer as there are gardeners; experiment a little and use what works best for you. However, as a guideline for beginners, you can mix some bulb booster such as 9-9-6 or flowering plant fertilizer such as 15-30-15 into the soil at the bottom of planting holes. You can also add a handful of bonemeal at this time— just remember that the smell of bonemeal

Hardy Bulb "To Do" List

Fall
- Purchase and plant new bulbs; replant bulbs that were placed in nursery beds while their foliage ripened.
- Label areas where bulbs are planted to prevent inadvertent digging/damage.
- Fertilize existing bulb plantings with a bulb booster (e.g., 9-9-6) or a flowering plant fertilizer (e.g., 15-30-15).
- Keep bulbs watered until freeze-up.

Winter
- Force bulbs such as paperwhites and hyacinths for indoor enjoyment.

Spring
- Fertilize bulbs as they start into active growth, just after the ground has thawed; use compost, a flowering plant fertilizer (e.g., 15-30-15), or any one of several available bulb fertilizers (e.g., 4-10-8, 7-10-5).
- Enjoy your bulbs as they brighten the spring garden.
- Water regularly to keep soil moist at all times.
- Deadhead early-blooming species and cultivars as their blossoms fade.
- Fertilize again after the flowers have died.
- Let bulb foliage ripen and die without interference.
- If desired, transplant bulbs either into nursery beds while their foliage ripens or to another part of the garden if your evolving garden plan requires it.

Summer
- Continue to deadhead.
- Continue to let bulb foliage ripen.
- Pull dead bulb foliage when it can be removed without resistance and add it to the compost pile.
- Cut back on water for the bulbs' sake, although if other perennials share their space, water them as required; dormant bulbs will usually not suffer if thirsty neighbors pick up the slack.

might attract dogs, raccoons, skunks, and other critters that are partial to digging for bones! For established plantings of hardy bulbs, work a flowering plant fertilizer (e.g., 15-30-15) or a bulb booster (e.g., 9-9-6) into the soil in early fall to encourage bulb replenishment and flower bud formation. For tender and hardy bulbs, apply a so-called bulb fertilizer, such as 4-10-8, 7-10-5, 5-10-5, or 5-10-10, or a flowering plant fertilizer such as 15-30-15 when bulbs start growing in spring and again when they have finished blooming. In parts of the prairies where the soil is rich in potassium, low-potassium fertilizers such as 11-48-0 or 16-20-0 should provide adequate bulb nutrition.

Mulching

Bulbs, like all plants on the prairies, are well served with an application of year-round organic mulch. Not only does organic mulch conserve moisture in the soil, regulate soil temperature, and suppress weeds, it also adds nutrients, improving soil texture and composition as it decomposes. Mature compost, shredded leaves, leaf mold, dried grass clippings, and various shredded bark products are all good choices. They are readily penetrated by water, but not so lightweight that they are easily blown about by the wind. Maintain organic mulches to a depth of 8 to 10 cm (3 to 4 in.), topping them up periodically as they decompose and are incorporated into the soil. Tiny bulbs only require a thin layer of mulch, 2.5 to 5 cm (1 to 2 in.) deep.

A year-round blanket of organic mulch on bulb beds conserves moisture, prevents weeds, moderates fluctuations in soil temperature, and adds important nutrients to the soil. *Lesley Reynolds*

Staking

Tall varieties of lilies, gladiolas, and dahlias all benefit from staking, especially in windy areas. Although not very esthetically pleasing, the best time to insert stakes is at the time of planting, to avoid damaging the bulbs later on when they are buried out of sight. Also, it is better to have stakes in use before wind damage occurs to delicate stems; staking a plant once it has been harmed is a tricky business at best and never very satisfactory.

Choose stakes that are a little shorter than the anticipated mature size of the plant, tuck them in on the windward side, and tie the plants loosely with soft twine, horticultural tape, or long plastic twist ties sold especially for this

Arching bent willow canes are attractive supports for top-heavy lilies.
Lesley Reynolds

purpose. Allow the plants to lean slightly as they would be inclined to do when left to their own devices. Staking plants absolutely vertically gives them an unnatural look; it is the rare plant that grows perfectly upright in nature.

Deadheading and Ripening Foliage

Bulbs benefit from deadheading as soon as they stop blooming. This entails removing spent blossoms and their stems down to the first leaves with scissors or a sharp knife, to prevent energy from being directed to seed production when it can be put to better use replenishing the bulb's food supply. However, if you would like some of the minor bulbs such as glory-of-the-snow, striped and Siberian squill, and grape hyacinth to increase their spread through self-seeding, leave their faded blossoms intact so they can produce the necessary seeds.

What to do with the dying foliage of bulbs that have perennialized in the garden is another matter. No matter how tempted you are to get rid of bulb foliage the moment it begins to deteriorate, don't! Instead, wait until the foliage has died back completely before removing it. This is important because a bulb's energy supply is much depleted by the time it has finished blooming, and it needs its leaves to manufacture next year's food supply in the bulb. When a bulb is deprived of its capability to produce food too early, its performance the following year will be the poorer for it. Nor is it a good idea to braid, knot, or tie up the leaves— although this looks tidier, it too interferes with food production by reducing the amount of exposed leaf surface available for photosynthesis. The time to deal with bulb foliage is when it has completely withered to yellow or brown, and can be removed with no resistance by a simple twist of the wrist.

Most gardeners dislike the look of dying bulb foliage and try to disguise it, with varying degrees of success, among large-leaved perennials such as lady's mantle, hosta, and geranium (see Chapter 3, p. 17, Perennials to Hide Dying Spring Bulb Foliage). Other gardeners actually transplant bulbs, foliage and all, into out-of-the-way nursery beds to let the foliage ripen and the bulbs rejuvenate, and then replant them into perennial and mixed borders at the usual time in the fall.

Tender Bulb "To Do" List

Spring
- Buy new bulbs.
- To give them a head start, plant new bulbs in pots, water, and grow them indoors under grow lights for six weeks before moving them outside when all threat of frost has passed.
- Check stored bulbs for fungal disease, drying, and signs of new growth.
- Discard diseased or shriveled bulbs.
- When stored bulbs start sprouting, or at the appropriate time (see individual plant descriptions), separate them if necessary, plant them in pots, resume watering, and grow under grow lights until it is time to move them outside.
- Transplant bulbs that were started indoors into the garden or move pots outside when all threat of frost has passed.

- Bulbs not given a head start indoors can be planted directly outdoors one to two weeks before the last expected frost date.
- Fertilize with compost, a flowering plant fertilizer (e.g., 15-30-15), or any one of several available bulb fertilizers (e.g., 4-10-8, 7-10-5) at the time of planting.

Summer
- Keep bulbs moist.
- Stake tall gladiolas and dahlias before wind and rain damage occurs.
- Fertilize with a flowering plant fertilizer (e.g., 15-30-15) on a regular basis throughout the summer.
- Be vigilant for slug and aphid attacks; deal with infestations immediately.
- Be prepared to move potted specimens to a sheltered spot if cold nighttime temperatures threaten.

- Resist the temptation to remove ripening foliage until it is completely dead; this often doesn't occur for tender bulbs until after the first hard frost.

Fall
- Lift, label, dry, and store tender bulbs.
- Do not separate bulbs until spring, just before planting.
- If you wish, treat bulbs with a fungicide and (or) insecticide to avoid potential problems during storage.

Winter
- Check stored bulbs periodically for disease and shriveling.
- Discard diseased bulbs or those that have shriveled beyond salvation.
- Maintain moisture levels in the packing medium for bulbs that require it.

Pests and Diseases

By and large, bulbs grown on the prairies are relatively pest and disease free. Rodents and deer are probably the biggest troublemakers, although aphids and slugs also sometimes cause gardeners to despair, and botrytis, viruses, and fungal disease occasionally rear their ugly heads. These headaches can be prevented or minimized by buying healthy bulbs, providing the growing conditions they prefer, and keeping a clean garden. Most often, cultural solutions can be found for these problems, but if they don't work to your satisfaction, check with your local garden center or provincial/state horticulturist for current, registered chemical solutions.

Rodent/Deer Resistant Bulbs
Agapanthus (lily-of-the-Nile)
Allium (ornamental onion)
Anemonella (rue anemone)
Arisaema (Jack-in-the-pulpit)
Caladium (fancy-leaved caladium)
Camassia (camass)
Colchicum (autumn crocus)
Convallaria (lily-of-the-valley)
Corydalis (tuberous corydalis)
Crinum (crinum lily)
Dahlia (dahlia)
Eranthis (winter aconite)
Erythronium (dog's-tooth violet)
Fritillaria (fritillary)
Galanthus (snowdrop)
Galtonia (summer hyacinth)
Hyacinthus (hyacinth)
Hymenocallis (spider lily)
Muscari (grape hyacinth)
Narcissus (daffodil)
Nectaroscordum (nectaroscordum)
Nerine (Guernsey lily)
Ornithogalum (star-of-Bethlehem)
Oxalis (wood sorrel)
Ranunculus (Persian buttercup)
Sanguinaria (bloodroot)
Scilla (squill)
Zantedeschia (calla lily)
Zephyranthes (fairy lily)

- **Rodents and deer.** The best way to deter marauding rodents and deer is to plant species that do not appeal to them. Narcissus, for example, are given a wide berth by most creatures because they are poisonous. On the other hand, tulips are considered a great delicacy and are usually the first bulbs to disappear when furry, four-legged friends come for a visit. To foil subterranean attacks by voles, moles, and gophers, sink wire- or plastic-mesh baskets topped with mesh lids into the flowerbeds and plant bulbs inside them. These will also trick squirrels and chipmunks who usually launch their bulb raids from above.

If squirrels and chipmunks dig up your bulbs in fall on a regular basis, consider this. Squirrels often come upon bulbs by accident when they are burying nuts for winter, most often in soil that has been recently worked, that is, where bulbs have been freshly planted! So, to avoid disappointment, spread a thick layer of mulch after you have planted your bulbs and cover that with anchored wire mesh of some sort (an old screen works well) to prevent ready access. Once the soil has settled, squirrels are far less likely to discover your precious bulbs.

Short of making prisoners of blooming bulbs in wire cages, there is very little that you can do to prevent deer from dining in your garden. Many people have developed coping strategies that work for them under certain circumstances (fences, bags of human hair, soap, blood meal, mothballs, motion detectors, etc.), but all are quite labor intensive, either to construct or to replenish after rain or overhead watering, and not one of them is foolproof (except maybe the fence, if it is high enough and the gates are always kept closed). If deer are regular visitors to your garden (you should be so lucky!), then just accept that as long as you insist on planting bulbs that are to their liking (e.g., tulips) they are going to like eating them.

Checkered lily (*Fritillaria meleagris*) is one of many deer and rodent resistant bulbs available to prairie gardeners.
Lesley Reynolds

- **Aphids and slugs.** Aphids, which come in all colors, are little sapsuckers that cause bud distortion, stunting, and loss of vigor in plants. They can also infest the bulbs themselves. Be vigilant; early detection followed by applying a forceful stream of water to affected plants on a regular basis are important elements of aphid control. Insecticidal soaps, applied according to the instructions on the bottle, can also be effective.

  Slugs—is there a prairie garden without them? Large holes chewed in otherwise healthy foliage and slimy mucous trails on the soil or pathways are the telltale signs of these creatures that gardeners love to hate. Handpicking them in the evening, early morning, or after a rainfall, when they are most active, is the best way to keep the upper hand. However, baiting, spreading diatomaceous earth or ground egg shells around susceptible plants, surrounding plants with a copper collar, and poisoning are other control techniques that gardeners use at one time or another. Take your pick!

- **Fungal disease and viruses.** Botrytis, or gray mold, is a fungal disease that generally takes hold in humid conditions and manifests itself through small yellowish brown spots on the foliage that eventually turn gray. Begonias, lilies, and some tulips are especially susceptible to botrytis. Maintaining good air circulation is the key to preventing it, but should it develop, immediately discard the infected leaves, or the entire plant in severe cases. Dump diseased material in the garbage can, not the composter. Also clean up all foliage from infected plants at the end of the season so the fungus doesn't overwinter and reinfect plants in the spring. Some fungicides are available commercially to deal with botrytis.

Viruses, which are responsible for the attractive streaking in tulip blossoms that sent heads spinning and bank accounts plunging during seventeenth-century "Tulipomania," are not desirable. Besides the telltale streaking of flowers and foliage, viruses also cause stunting, weakening, deformed flowers, and eventual death in bulbs. What's more, they are contagious! If you suspect one of your bulbs is infected, discard it in the garbage and don't replant a virus-prone species in the same spot for several years. Viruses, including mosaic virus, are spread by aphids, so controlling aphid populations goes a long way towards preventing viral infections. They can also be spread by tools, such as knives, scissors, or pruning shears, that were used to cut infected flowers. To avoid spreading viruses to healthy plants, sanitize contaminated tools with a mixture of 100 mL (0.5 cup) bleach added to 1 L (4 cups) water.

Rots may be either fungal or bacterial in origin, and often arrive with newly purchased bulbs. Infected bulbs either do not grow at all, or produce weak, spindly, anemic foliage at best. Discard any suspicious-looking bulbs (soft, mushy ones or hard, dry ones) in the garbage can; provide healthy bulbs with good drainage. You can also dust bulbs with a fungicide at the time of planting to prevent rot.

- **Other pests.** A handful of other pests can wreak some havoc in bulb plantings, but their occurrence is rare on the prairies because of our dry climate, relatively cool summers, and frigid winters. Beetles and borers might feast on leaves, stems, or blossoms (handpick, remove infected parts, or spray with an insecticidal soap or insecticide). Maggots and wireworms can damage bulbs and roots (discard infected bulbs and practise "crop rotation"). Finally, mites might parasitize a bulb or two (control with a miticide) and thrips strike terror in the hearts of gladiola growers (discard affected plants and bulbs, treat infected plants with a systemic insecticide, store bulbs hosting hibernating thrips with naphthalene flakes or soak them in warm [43° C, 110° F] water for half an hour).

Lifting and Storing Tender Bulbs

Some tender bulbs, such as dahlias, gladiolas, begonias, and cannas, do not survive prairie winters and must be treated either as annuals, and replaced every year, or lifted from the garden and stored indoors during dormancy. Other tender bulbs, such as lily-of-the-Nile and crinum lily, also don't survive prairie winters, but they are evergreen and do not need a period of dormancy. Brought inside, pot and all, they will continue to grow without any interruption, given appropriate lighting and moisture.

The time for lifting tender bulbs is autumn, when their foliage has ripened to yellow or brown and after the first killing frost. Take the following steps to ensure success.

- Loosen the soil around the bulbs with a garden fork or spade, and then lift the whole clump—soil, bulbs, and all.
- Separate the bulbs by hand, brushing off any loose soil in the process.
- Remove foliage with a sharp knife.
- Dry bulbs outdoors in a shady, well-ventilated spot for a few days.
- Sort and label the bulbs.
- Dust the bulbs with a fungicide and (or) insecticide if you wish, especially if you've had trouble with fungus or insects in the past.
- Do not separate multiplying bulbs before storing; this helps prevent dehydration and the spread of disease.
- Bulbs with a protective sheath or tunic such as gladiolas can be stored directly in a paper or mesh bag, cardboard box, or wicker basket. A dry storage medium such as perlite, vermiculite, or peat moss can also be used to separate bulbs and thus prevent bruising and the spread of rot.
- Thin-skinned bulbs, such as dahlia and canna, need a bit of moisture in the storage medium to prevent drying and shriveling.
- Check stored bulbs periodically during the winter for rotting and dehydration; throw out any spoiled bulbs.
- Store bulbs in a cool, dry spot, such as a garage or basement, with temperatures maintained in the 2 to 13° C (35 to 55° F) range.
- If dormant tender bulbs have been grown in pots, cut back foliage and store the pots, bulbs and all, in a cool, dark garage or basement; resume watering in the spring when you see evidence of fresh growth.

Division and Propagation

Propagating plants, whether they are annuals, perennials, or bulbs, is a satisfying pastime for many gardeners. There are several reasons for producing your own horticultural offspring—saving money, sharing with friends, securing plants not readily available through regular venues, hybridizing, or simply "for the challenge."

When it comes to bulbs, some propagation techniques are straightforward and others are highly specialized. Regardless, gardeners are rarely blessed with "quick results" as most processes require a waiting time of several years before new bulbs are ready to bloom. This in turn necessitates vigilance, patience, effort, and room somewhere in the garden for a nursery bed where new bulbs can be coaxed to maturity before taking their rightful place in the garden.

Considering that time is a precious commodity for many people these days and that most bulbs are readily available and relatively inexpensive, it is a wonder that anyone still makes the effort to propagate bulbs. Nonetheless, there are dedicated gardeners who do and others who'd like to try, so here are some tips on the most common bulb propagation techniques.

In addition to generating new plant colonies, division has the benefit of rejuvenating and invigorating old ones. It's time to divide when clumps are overcrowded and flower production is in decline. Do it when the foliage starts to die back so plants have a chance to re-establish before winter arrives. Simply take a sharp spade or garden fork and loosen the soil around existing clumps, lift them, and pry them apart, using a knife if necessary. Select large healthy plants from the clumps and replant them in the border; grow the smaller ones in a nursery bed for a few years before giving them a permanent home. For specific planting guidelines, see Chapter 5: Planting Bulbs, p. 39.

- **True bulbs.** Healthy, well-nourished bulbs produce offsets, or bulblets, around their basal plate. Bulblets, each attached to a section of basal plate, can be gently separated from the parent bulb and replanted in the garden where they may take a few years to reach the necessary size for blooming. Some lilies produce small above-ground bulbs on stems in the leaf axils; these are called bulbils. When they are ready for planting, bulbils will easily detach from the stems.
- **Corms.** To propagate cormous plants such as crocus or autumn crocus, dig them up and separate the small offsets, called cormels, from the mother corm. Replant directly into the ground for hardy species, remembering that it may take a few years before the growing corms have enough energy stored to support blooming.

- **Rhizomes.** Plants that grow from rhizomes, such as iris, should be divided several weeks after flowering. For bearded irises, dig up the rhizomes, cut them into segments so that each has a fan of leaves attached, cut back the leaves to 8 cm (3 in.), and dust the cut rhizome surfaces with a fungicide as a precautionary measure if you wish. Replant them almost immediately, slightly below the soil surface. Split beardless irises when the number and quality of flowers diminish, or when plants begin to die out in the middle. Cut foliage back to about 30 cm (12 in.) and split the plants into sections, each with at least six growth points and a healthy clump of roots.
- **Tubers and tuberous roots.** Tuberous plants such as dahlias and begonias can be divided in the spring at the time of planting. Simply use a sharp knife to cut each tuber into sections, ensuring that each section has a visible growth point. Dry the tuber pieces in a warm place for a few days, dust them with bulb dust, and then replant.

7
Indoor Bulbs

A s summer wanes and frost nips at the gardens, prairie gardeners are busy planting bulbs in anticipation of spring. However, when selecting bulbs for fall planting, gardeners can also choose some to force for indoor bloom during those short winter days when the cheering color and fragrance of flowering bulbs are most appreciated.

Forcing is a procedure that encourages a plant to flower out of its normal season by simulating the natural conditions than trigger blooming. Many favorite spring-flowering bulbs are native to the northern hemisphere and need a winter equivalent—a cold, dark period—before they will burst into bloom indoors. Others, such as tender summer-flowering begonias, freesia, and ranunculus, and fall-blooming crocus and *Colchicum*, do not require cold periods to induce bloom.

Tulips, crocus, iris, daffodils, and several other charming bulbs that grace our spring gardens are ideal candidates for indoor bloom from December to April. Look for bulbs labeled as suitable for forcing, generally early-blooming varieties. Some bulbs are available pre-cooled by the producer, which will reduce, but not completely eliminate, cooling time.

Choose large, firm bulbs free of blemishes

Tulips, hyacinths, and narcissus are easy to force into bloom for indoor winter enjoyment. *Liesbeth Leatherbarrow*

57

or soft spots. If you are not planting them immediately, store them in a paper, not plastic, bag in a cool place. They may be refrigerated, but avoid storing them with ripening fruit or vegetables, which give off ethylene gas that damages the bulbs, especially their developing flower buds.

Before planting, plan the bloom schedule on a calendar, taking into account the various chilling times required by different bulbs. By staggering the start of the forcing process over several weeks in the fall, it's possible to have indoor blooms for most of the winter and early spring. If it's more convenient, plant all the pots at once and store them dry until it is time to chill them.

Shallow bulb pans allow for a striking display of forced bulbs; however, make sure that the container is at least twice as deep as the length of the bulbs to allow space for adequate root growth. Other types of clay and ceramic containers are also suitable for bulbs, provided they have drainage holes. Small, lightweight plastic pots do not suit top-heavy bulbs such as hyacinths, as they are prone to tipping over.

Best Bulbs for Forcing and their Cooling Periods

Many popular spring-flowering bulbs can be purchased in fall for indoor forcing. Cooling times are approximate and chilled bulbs should be checked regularly for root and shoot development.

Allium flavum, *A. karataviense*, *A. oreophilum* (ornamental onion) – 12 weeks
Anemone blanda (windflower) – 12 weeks
Chionodoxa luciliae (glory-of-the-snow) – 12 weeks
Convallaria (lily-of-the-valley) – purchase pre-chilled, or dig dormant rhizomes from garden and store in cool, dark place until you wish to start them
Crocus vernus (Dutch crocus) – 12 weeks
Eranthis (winter aconite) – 12 weeks
Fritillaria meleagris (checkered lily) – 12 weeks
Galanthus (snowdrop) – 12 weeks
Hyacinthus orientalis (hyacinth) – precooled

bulbs, 8 weeks; uncooled bulbs, 12 weeks
Iris (bulbous iris) – 12 weeks
Ixiolirion (ixia lily) – 12 weeks
Leucojum (snowflake) – 12 weeks
Muscari armeniacum (grape hyacinth) – 12 weeks
Narcissus (daffodil)
• small, early-flowering cultivars ('February Gold', 'Jack Snipe', and 'Tête à Tête') – 12 weeks
• Trumpet cultivars ('Dutch Master', 'Golden Harvest', 'Mount Hood') – 16 weeks
• Large-cupped or Long-cupped cultivars ('Carlton', 'Flower Record', 'Ice Follies') – 16 weeks
• Small-cupped or Short-cupped cultivars ('Barrett Browning') – 16 weeks

• Triandrus cultivars ('Thalia') – 16 weeks
• paperwhites ('Grand Soleil d'Or', 'Ziva') – no cooling period required
Oxalis adenophylla (wood sorrel) – 12 weeks
Puschkinia (striped squill) – 12 weeks
Scilla (squill) – 12 weeks
Tulipa (tulip) – 14 weeks
• Species tulips, including *Tulipa greigii* hybrids, *T. kaufmanniana* hybrids
• Single Early tulips ('Apricot Beauty', 'Christmas Dream')
• Double Early tulips ('Monte Carlo')
• Triumph tulips ('Golden Melody', 'Merry Widow')

Cover the drainage hole of your chosen container with a piece of broken pottery or a small piece of screen and add a sterile planting mix, putting in enough so that the tops of the bulbs will be 1.5 to 2.5 cm (0.5 to 1 in.) below the rim of the container. For the best display, plant as many bulbs as the container will hold, leaving 0.5 to 1.5 cm (0.25 to 0.5 in.) between the bulbs and 1.5 cm (0.5 in.) between the bulbs and the sides of the container. Plant tulip bulbs with the flat side of the bulb facing the side of the container. The first large leaves emerge from that side and will look best facing outward over the rim of the pot. Once the bulbs are set in place with the pointed tip up, add planting mix until only the tips of the bulbs are showing. Do not press the bulbs down or firm the planting mix; the bulbs need a loose growing medium to root properly. Small bulbs (e.g., crocus) may be covered with 1.5 cm (0.5 in.) of planting mix. It's best to stick to one type of bulb per container; even if you combine bulbs with similar chilling times, they may not all bloom at the same time.

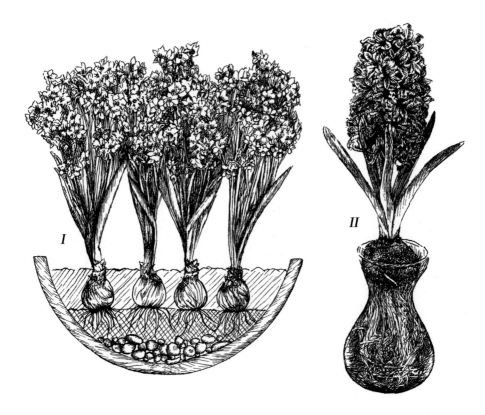

Many fragrant spring-flowering bulbs are easy to force indoors in water. I. *Narcissus papyraceus* (paperwhites) in a sand and pebble-filled container. II. *Hyacinthus* (hyacinth) in a forcing glass.

For a lush display of flowers, try planting two layers of bulbs in a container at least 20 cm (8 in.) deep. Fill the container half full of planting mix, set a layer of bulbs in place, then fill with planting mix so that just the bulb tips show. Plant a second layer of bulbs in the spaces between the first layer, and add planting mix.

Once the bulbs are planted, label the pots with the bulb variety and date planted. Water the bulbs thoroughly, draining off excess water, and store them in a cool, dark place at a temperature between 3 and 10° C (35 and 50° F). The cooling site can be a refrigerator, cold storage room, or garage where temperatures will stay above freezing. Place the pots in a plastic bag, leaving the bag open, to keep the planting medium from drying out. It should be kept slightly damp, but not wet. If necessary, cover pots stored in garages or cold storage rooms with newspaper or a cardboard box to keep out the light. The length of the chilling period will depend on the type of bulb; they will be ready to move into warmer temperatures when they have developed a healthy root mass and shoots have grown to between 2.5 and 5 cm (1 and 2 in.).

At this time, move the pots to a cool, moderately lit location where the temperature does not exceed 16° C (60° F), watering frequently and feeding with a half-strength houseplant fertilizer. When flower buds appear, move the pots to a brighter but still cool location. If they are subjected to overly warm temperatures prematurely, the flowers may fail to open. When the flower buds show color, move the pots to a location at room temperature with bright indirect light; however, flowers will last longer if the temperature is kept on the cool side. Turn containers regularly so all leaves receive enough light.

Bulbs that do not need chilling to induce bloom can be planted as above and kept in a cool location (16° C, 60° F). Move them to a location at room temperature when the buds begin to show color.

After the bulbs have finished blooming, remove the flower stems and move the pots into direct sunlight. Once the foliage has ripened and died back naturally, the bulbs may be lifted and stored in a cool, dry place and planted in the garden in the fall. They cannot be forced twice, but will sometimes rebloom in the garden.

Hyacinths, crocus, and paperwhites may also be grown in water in hourglass-shaped vases. The bulb rests in the top section of the vase and the roots grow into the bottom; different sizes of vases are available to accommodate both large and small bulbs. Look for hyacinth and crocus bulbs that have been pre-cooled for this purpose; paperwhites do not require chilling. Because some of these plants, especially large-bloomed hyacinths, can become top heavy, it is a good idea to fill the bottom level of the vase with decorative stone chips to make it more stable. Fill the vase with water to touch the base of the bulb and place it in a cool, dark location. Check periodically to make sure the roots are in water, and change the water weekly. When a healthy root mass has formed and the bulbs have sprouted, move the vase to a cool, but brighter location until the buds are ready to open. Hyacinths and crocuses require a longer period than paperwhites to establish roots. Discard bulbs forced in water after they have bloomed since they will not flower again.

Growing bulbs indoors is an ideal winter project for children. Paperwhites are among the easiest bulbs to force—simply place them in a container without drainage holes on top of a layer of decorative stones, pebbles, coarse sand, or thoroughly moistened vermiculite. Add enough water to touch the bottom of the bulbs and set the container in a cool, bright room. The fragrant flowers will appear in about four to six weeks.

8 Bulbs for Prairie Gardens

The best bulbs for prairie gardens are described in this chapter. They are divided into three categories: hardy, borderline (for adventurous gardeners), and tender. Each plant entry includes a "Plant at a Glance" summary—a quick review of a plant's characteristics and cultural requirements. Plants are classified by bulb type, and approximate flowering times are given; expect bloom times to vary slightly depending on your location and the weather in any particular year. Height dimensions that represent the expected rate of growth, provided the plant's cultural requirements are met, are also given. Plant size will vary from garden to garden, depending on soil, light, and microclimate.

Soil preferences are indicated as average or fertile, and in some cases, amendments such as organic material or sand are suggested. Moisture and drainage requirements are also noted; however, except for a few woodland species, all bulbs require good drainage.

Light requirements are specified as full sun (over eight hours of direct sun per day), part sun (four to eight hours of direct sun per day), light shade (less than four hours of direct sun per day or bright filtered light), and full shade (no direct unfiltered sunlight).

Planting time, depth, and spacing, plus any special planting instructions are included together with an indication of whether the bulb is poisonous, deer and rodent resistant, or good for forcing. Suggestions are also made for where to grow each bulb and what to plant with it.

For general advice on designing with bulbs, bulb purchasing, planting, and maintenance, please refer to Chapters 1 through 7.

Hardy Bulbs

Most of the bulbs grown in prairie gardens are hardy, that is, they require a cold dormant period and are tough enough to survive a prairie winter, given the right microclimate. There are many superb hardy bulbs that can thrive in prairie gardens, but a large number of them are highly underused or underappreciated. The majority of hardy bulbs are perennials, and so will provide pleasure year after year—most in spring, but some in summer or fall. The hardy bulbs described next are all excellent choices for prairie gardens.

Allium
(*al*-ee-um)
ornamental onion

PLANT AT A GLANCE (photos pp. 16, 17, 25, 65)

Type: true bulb
Flowering Time: late spring to mid-summer, depending on the species
Height: 15 to 150 cm (0.5 to 5 ft.)
Soil: fertile, moist, well drained
Light: full to part sun
When to Plant: fall
How to Plant: depth variable, depending on the size of the bulb—see individual entries; space small species 10 to 15 cm (4 to 6 in.) apart, large species 20 to 30 cm (8 to 12 in.) apart
Propagation: offsets, seed (also self-seeds)
Poisonous: no
Deer/Rodent Resistant: yes
Good for Forcing: yes, small species only

Onions, leeks, scallions, and chives have been grown for highly practical culinary and medicinal purposes since the earliest days of civilization; for centuries, however, no thought was given to growing these or other alliums for their highly ornamental value. Today's gardeners know better, as they revel in the exceptional beauty and sheer drama of alliums, both tall and small, in perennial and mixed borders.

Ornamental alliums are excellent for bridging the gap between spring- and summer-flowering bulbs. As many tulips and narcissus begin to fade and before lily, dahlia, and gladiola blossoms emerge, sparkling clusters of starry allium blossoms take center stage in borders and rock gardens. Alliums' unique shape, regal bearing, and majestic appearance conjure up images of an exotic Middle Eastern ancestry. Indeed, many alliums do originate in the Middle East, so the image is an appropriate one.

Portrait

Alliums produce a whole range of leaf shapes, from strappy and erect, to narrow and cylindrical, to broad and spreading. For many species, the foliage has withered by the time flowering occurs, earning these plants the nickname of drumstick allium. Also, as one might expect, allium foliage emits a pungent, onionlike scent when bruised or crushed.

Allium flowers, however, can be sweetly scented and come in shades of pink, purple, white, yellow, blue, and even dark maroon, depending on the species. The species also determines the shape of the flower (star- or bell-shaped) and how the flowers are arranged, whether in a loose, nodding cluster or a tight globe shape of either small or huge proportions. Some allium flower globes achieve an impressive diameter of 25 cm (10 in.) or

Allium aflatunense 'Purple Sensation' (ornamental onion). *Ken Girard*

Allium cernuum (nodding or wild onion). *Liesbeth Leatherbarrow*

Allium flavum (ornamental onion). *Ken Girard*

Allium karataviense (ornamental onion). *Liesbeth Leatherbarrow*

more. However, unless they are pampered after blooming, their bulbs decline in vigor and the flower cluster size diminishes accordingly. Actually, all alliums have the potential for declining in vigor if they are planted too densely, so give them plenty of elbow room to avoid disappointment.

A number of novelty alliums have been developed as giant showstoppers, and are worth replacing every few years, should they start shrinking. Both 'Globemaster' and *Allium christophii* generate mighty flower clusters with a diameter of 25 cm (10 in.); 'Mount Everest' clusters measure in at a respectable 15 cm (6 in.).

Whether or not to deadhead alliums poses a conundrum for gardeners. On the one hand, dried flower clusters are attractive in the garden year-round and provide a tasty snack for birds in winter. On the other hand, they self-seed like crazy and every seed germinates, resulting in a veritable carpet of allium seedlings that need pulling the following spring.

- *Allium aflatunense* (90 cm, 36 in.) produces spectacular 10-cm (4-in.), starburst globes of lavender flowers on bare, ribbed stalks, after its blue-green foliage has faded. 'Purple Sensation', a popular cultivar, is violet in color. Planting depth: 10 cm (4 in.).
- *Allium atropurpureum* (90 cm, 36 in.) produces a flat, 8-cm (3-in.) cluster of deep wine purple, star-shaped flowers on stiff stems. This is not a consistent bloomer on the prairies. Planting depth: 5 to 8 cm (2 to 3 in.).
- *Allium bulgaricum*. See *Nectaroscordum* (p. 112).
- *Allium caeruleum* (syn. *A. azureum*) (60 cm, 24 in.), blue globe onion, produces compact, cornflower-blue, globe-shaped flower clusters on erect stems. Planting depth: 5 cm (2 in.).
- *Allium cernuum* (45 cm, 18 in.), nodding or wild onion, is a North American native and produces narrow, strap-shaped, dark green leaves and stiff stems that curl at the top, bearing loose, drooping clusters of small, dark pink, bell-shaped flowers. Planting depth: 5 cm (2 in.).
- *Allium christophii* (syn. *A. albopilosum*) (60 cm, 24 in.), star of Persia, produces shiny, broad strappy foliage and sturdy, 60-cm (24-in.) flower stalks, each topped with an incredible 30-cm (12-in.) globe of over a hundred tiny, perfectly star-shaped flowers radiating from a central point. The blossoms are pale mauve with an exquisite metallic iridescence. Planting depth: 15 to 20 cm (6 to 8 in.).
- *Allium flavum* (30 to 45 cm, 12 to 18 in.) produces loose clusters of bright yellow, sweetly scented, bell-shaped flowers with prominent stamens; the cylindrical foliage is gray-green. Planting depth: 5 cm (2 in.).

- *Allium giganteum* (1.5 to 2 m, 5 to 6.5 ft.) produces medium green, strap-shaped foliage and dense 10-cm (4-in.) clusters of lovely lilac pink, star-shaped flowers with prominent stamens. Plant in a sheltered location. Planting depth: 15 cm (6 in.).
- *Allium karataviense* (15 cm, 6 in.) has a grapefruit-sized globe of tiny, lilac blue flowers nestled in broad gray-green, crimson-tinted foliage. Planting depth: 10 cm (4 in.).
- *Allium moly* (45 cm, 18 in.), golden garlic or lily leek, produces loose clusters of lemon yellow, star-shaped flowers above paired, lance-shaped, green leaves. Planting depth: 5 cm (2 in.).
- *Allium oreophilum* (syn. *A. ostrow-skianum*) (20 cm, 8 in.) produces loose clusters of bell-shaped, rose-purple flowers above linear, medium green leaves. Planting depth: 5 cm (2 in.).
- *Allium schoenoprasum* (60 cm, 24 in.), chives, produces a dense clump of narrow, cylindrical edible leaves, and small globes of pale purple to pink flowers; 'Profusion'™ is a sterile cultivar. Planting depth: 5 cm (2 in.).
- *Allium tuberosum* (50 cm, 20 in.), garlic or Chinese chives, forms clumps of solid, edible linear leaves and large umbels of fragrant, white, star-shaped flowers in late summer. Planting depth: 5 cm (2 in.).

> **Allium Lore**
>
> - According to Homer, the ancient Greek poet, magical properties of *Allium moly* protected Odysseus against all harm in the lair of the sorceress Circe.
> - Garlic supposedly gave strength to the Egyptian pyramid builders and courage to Roman soldiers.
> - In southern Europe of long ago, the common folk regarded alliums as a source of good luck and protection against demons.
> - In the Middle Ages, members of the onion family were used to ward off evil spirits, the plague, and infection.
> - Early American settlers strapped garlic cloves to the feet of smallpox victims in an effort to cure them.

Where to Grow
There is an allium suitable for every garden circumstance. The small, very low-growing alliums such as *Allium karataviense* and *A. oreophilum* are naturals for planting in a rock garden. Short *A. flavum* and *A. moly* are logical choices for naturalizing or massing in borders. Clusters of tall alliums such as *A. aflatunense* and *A. giganteum*, not to mention the giants 'Globemaster' and 'Mount Everest', definitely add drama to mixed and perennial borders.

Perfect Partners
Alliums look best when paired with bushy plants that hide fading foliage and soften the lines of bare flower stalks. Fern-leaf peony (*Paeonia tenuifolia*), geraniums, lady's mantle (*Alchemilla mollis*), lavender (*Lavandula*

spp.), and catmint (*Nepeta* spp.) are good choices, as are blue flax (*Linum perenne*), lilies (*Lilium* spp.), and false sunflowers (*Heliopsis helianthoides*). The combination of roses (*Rosa* spp.) and alliums is also an attractive one.

Anemonella
(ah-nem-oh-*nell*-uh)
rue anemone

PLANT AT A GLANCE (photo this page)

Type: tuber
Flowering Time: late spring
Height: 15 cm (6 in.)
Soil: fertile, moist, well drained
Light: part sun
When to Plant: fall (bare tubers), by mid-September at the latest; spring through fall (container-grown plants)
How to Plant: 5 to 8 cm (2 to 3 in.) deep, 30 cm (12 in.) apart; tubers dry out very easily, so as soon as you receive them, place in luke-warm water and soak for twenty-four hours, and then plant immediately, otherwise blooms may be sparse or non-existent
Propagation: division, seed (also self-seeds)
Poisonous: no
Deer/Rodent Resistant: yes
Good for Forcing: no

Rue anemone, or *Anemonella thalictroides*, is a dainty little woodland gem that puts on a restrained but elegant show for several weeks in spring. When viewed from close quarters, it is apparent that its flowers are diminutive copies of anemone blossoms (hence, *Anemonella*) and its intricately formed leaves bear a strong resemblance to those of meadow rue or *Thalictrum* (hence, *thalictroides*). Slow to establish, these clump-forming perennials grow from tiny, dahlialike tubers and are

White *Anemonella thalictroides* (rue anemone) and purple *A. thalic troides* 'Schoaf's Double'. *Llyn Strelau*

native to eastern North America. Given the conditions they prefer, they are also long-lived in the shady nooks and crannies of prairie gardens.

Portrait

Rue anemone produces delicate, fernlike compound leaves that consist of two- or three-lobed blue-green leaflets on fine, wiry stems. The fragile-looking, cup-shaped flowers form loose clusters at the ends of slender stems and, at 2 cm (0.75 in.) across, make a big impression compared to the small mound of soft foliage. The flowers of the species are white or palest pink, but several cultivars have been introduced in shades of white, pink, and greenish white; a number even have distinctive double blossoms.

Arisaema consanguineum (Jack-in-the-pulpit) (see p. 70). *Llyn Strelau*

Although sometimes hard to come by, the following cultivars are worth searching out for their unique beauty: 'Cameo' (double pale rose), 'Double Green' (double light green), 'Pink Full Double' (double pink), 'Green Dragon' (single green), 'Green Hurricane' (double green), 'Jade Feather' (double green), 'Rosea' (single rose pink, self-seeds true), 'Rubra Plena' (double dark pink), 'Schoaf's Double' (double pink, most readily available), 'White Full Double' (very rare double white).

If allowed to dry out, rue anemone may go dormant in late summer, but will happily reappear the following spring.

Where to Grow

Rue anemone is an excellent little plant for populating shady rock gardens or carpeting a woodland garden floor. It is also suitable for planting under deciduous shrubs in a mixed or shrub border. Because rue anemone is small and delicate looking, place it at the edge of a pathway or towards the front of a border where it will be noticed and enjoyed.

Combine rue anemone with other low-growing woodland plants for a natural look. Suitable partners include wild ginger (*Asarum canadensis*), foamflower (*Tiarella cordifolia*), bunchberry (*Cornus canadensis*), and small ferns such as the maidenhair fern (*Adiantum pedatum*).

Arisaema
(air-ih-*see*-mah)
Jack-in-the-pulpit

PLANT AT A GLANCE (photo p. 69)

Type: tuber
Flowering Time: late spring to early summer
Height: 30 to 60 cm (12 to 24 in.)
Soil: fertile, moist
Light: full shade to part sun
When to Plant: fall (bare tubers); spring through fall (container-grown plants)
How to Plant: 5 to 8 cm (2 to 3 in.) deep, 25 to 30 cm (10 to 12 in.) apart
Propagation: division, offsets, seed
Poisonous: yes, all parts harmful when ingested raw, bulbs edible when cooked
Deer/Rodent Resistant: yes
Good for Forcing: no

A most unusual-looking plant with its cobralike, hooded-leaf arrangement, Jack-in-the-pulpit has a quiet presence in woodland or shady gardens. Its understated elegance in shades of green is easy to overlook in the spring, but clusters of brilliant red berries in late summer and fall are definitely eye catching, a last hurrah in the garden before winter sets in.

The genus name *Arisaema* derives in part from the Latin *haema*, meaning blood red, and refers, of course, to the bright red color of the berries.

Jack-in-the-pulpit is an eastern North American wildflower that populates damp, shaded areas. Although poisonous when raw, North American Natives learned to cook the fleshy tubers and ate them with no ill side effects; as such, these "Indian turnips" were a staple Native food source.

One aspect of Jack-in-the-pulpit and other *Arisaemas* is fairly unique in the plant kingdom. Some plants are male, some are female, some are both, and some change back and forth. Usually *Arisaemas* are male when young. When they've built up enough energy in their tubers to reproduce, they switch, become female, and set fruit, only to revert back to the world of males the following year.

Portrait

The dignified Jack-in-the-pulpit produces single or paired, gracefully divided, three-lobed leaves. Spotted stems support the pulpit, a large, funnel-shaped, hooded, modified leaf, called the spathe, which in turn shelters Jack, a central stalk bearing the plant's reproductive parts, called the spadix. The complex flower arrangement of spathe and spadix gives this plant its unique appearance.

The cowl-like spathe is usually a plain green on the outside but can be flushed or striped brownish purple or white on the inside. The spadix, often colored a similar brownish purple, attracts pollinators.

As the flowers fade, the spathe withers and eventually disappears altogether, and the spadix forms clusters of red seeds that bring to mind a small ear of corn.

Although Jack-in-the-pulpit (*Arisaema triphyllum*) is by far the hardiest of the Arisaemas for prairie gardens, *A. consanguineum*, *A. candidissimum*, and *A. sikokianum* have also been grown successfully; all should be planted in sheltered spots and given winter protection.

Where to Grow

Jack-in-the-pulpit is an ideal woodland plant that thrives in dappled shade, but also works in a shaded border, especially in a wild or semi-wild planting scheme. Because its curious shape makes it a conversation piece, plant it where it can be readily seen by visitors—beside a woodland path is perfect.

Given the conditions he prefers, jaunty Jack may self-seed into a small colony, but a rampant spreader? Never!

Perfect Partners

Jack-in-the-pulpit looks most at home in a garden setting when interplanted with other leafy native woodland plants such as foamflower (*Tiarella cordifolia*), twinleaf (*Jeffersonia diphylla*), fairy bells (*Disporum trachycarpum*), and merrybells (*Uvularia grandiflora*, *U. sessifolia*).

Bulbocodium
(bul-bo-*co*-dee-um)
spring meadow saffron, mountain saffron

PLANT AT A GLANCE (photo p. 72)

Type: corm
Flowering Time: early spring
Height: 8 cm (3 in.)
Soil: average to fertile, well drained

Light: full to part sun
When to Plant: fall
How to Plant: 8 cm (3 in.) deep, 10 cm (4 in.) apart
Propagation: division, offsets, seed
Poisonous: no
Deer/Rodent Resistant: no
Good for Forcing: no

The genus *Bulbocodium*, closely related to *Colchicum*, consists of two species of cormous plants native to the alpine meadows, slopes, and grasslands of southern and eastern Europe, including the Alps and the Pyrenees. Only one of these species, *B. vernum*, is available to gardeners, and even this dainty little plant is not always easy to find. This is unfortunate because given the proper growing conditions, it is perfectly hardy on the prairies and, as one of the few pink early-flowering bulbs, makes a fine addition to a small bulb collection.

Bulbocodium vernum (spring meadow saffron). *Lesley Reynolds*

Portrait
Spring meadow saffron bears bright pinkish purple, widely funnel-shaped flowers up to 4 cm (1.5 in.) across that resemble small colchicums. Each corm produces up to three very short-stemmed flowers composed of six straplike tepals (petals and sepals) that open wide as the flowers mature in the spring sunshine. Short, narrow leaves hide beneath the flowers on each corm, and lengthen after blooming has finished.

Where to Grow
Spring meadow saffron is most at home tucked into rock gardens, but it is also suitable for naturalizing in the lawn. Plant small drifts of it with other early spring bulbs at the front of a border or beside a pathway.

Perfect Partners
Pink spring meadow saffron looks terrific beside deep blue Siberian squill (*Scilla sibirica*) and blue or purple *Iris reticulata*. It is also delightful grouped with white snow crocuses (*Crocus chrysanthus* 'Snow Bunting'),

snowdrops (*Galanthus* spp.), glory-of-the snow (*Chionodoxa luciliae*), and striped squill (*Puschkinia scilloides*). In the rock garden, combine it with low-growing perennials such as moss phlox (*Phlox subulata*) or rock cress *(Arabis caucasica)* that will fill in and bloom later in the spring.

Chionodoxa
(key-on-oh-*dox*-ah)
glory-of-the-snow

PLANT AT A GLANCE (photos p. 24, this page)

Type: true bulb
Flowering Time: early to mid-spring
Height: 20 cm (8 in.)
Soil: average to fertile, moist, well drained
Light: full to part sun
When to Plant: fall
How to Plant: 8 cm (3 in.) deep, 5 cm (2 in.) apart
Propagation: division, offsets, seed (also self-seeds)
Poisonous: no
Deer/Rodent Resistant: no
Good for Forcing: yes

The delicate blue sprays of starry *Chionodoxa*, or glory-of-the-snow, are a delightful sight beneath trees or shrubs in an informal spring landscape. Glory-of-the-snow is adaptable and hardy and enhances any prairie garden. Native to the mountain meadows of Crete, Cyprus, and Turkey, this genus was named in the nineteenth century by Swiss botanist Pierre Boissier, who found the plants growing in the Boz Dag (Tmolus) Mountains of western Turkey. When Boissier discovered the dainty blue flowers blooming near the melting snow, he named them from the Greek words *chion* (snow) and *doxa* (glory); the species name *luciliae* honors his wife Lucile.

Chionodoxa luciliae (glory-of-the-snow). Liesbeth Leatherbarrow

There is much confusion regarding the nomenclature of this hardy little bulb. The most readily available glory-of-the-snow has long been sold as *Chionodoxa luciliae* (syn. *C. gigantea*); however, this plant is likely *C. forbesii* (syn. *C. siehei*), since the true *C. luciliae* named by Boissier bears fewer flowers per stem than the plant commonly found in gardens. Opinions differ on the true identities of these species, and it is likely that both, and possibly even more, species have found their way into North American gardens. Ultimately, all that gardeners need to remember is that bulbs labeled *C. luciliae*, *C. gigantea*, *C. forbesii*, or *C. siehei* should be hardy on the prairies.

As a further curiosity, there is a naturally occuring hybrid of *Chionodoxa forbesii* and *Scilla bifolia* named x *Chionoscilla allenii*. Both parent bulbs are hardy on the prairies, so it is possible to dabble in plant breeding by planting them side by side and selecting the resultant hybrid seedlings.

Portrait

Glory-of-the-snow bears racemes of six-petaled, star-shaped flowers measuring 1 to 2 cm (0.5 to 0.75 in.) across. There are only two linear, medium green basal leaves per bulb, which are unobtrusive once blooming has ceased.

- *Chionodoxa forbesii* (syn. *C. siehei*) (20 cm, 8 in.) produces up to twelve purple-blue, white-centered flowers per stem. The blooms on this species are outward facing. 'Alba' is a white selection, and the vigorous cultivar 'Pink Giant' has pink flowers with white centers.
- *Chionodoxa luciliae* (syn. *C. gigantea*) (15 cm, 6 in.) has up to three pale lavender-blue, white-centered flowers on each stem; the blooms are upfacing.

Where to Grow

Glory-of-the-snow is perfect for naturalizing beneath deciduous trees and shrubs in woodland gardens, as it will bloom before the trees have leafed out and, with any luck, self-seed to form substantial colonies. It is also at home in rock gardens, at the front of borders or along pathways, and naturalized in lawns with other small early spring-blooming bulbs.

Perfect Partners

Glory-of-the-snow blooms at the same time as many early species tulips. Try blue or white varieties with the species tulips *Tulipa tarda* and *T. turkestanica*, or with red tulips like *T. greigii* 'Red Riding Hood'. Pink glory-of-the-snow shows up beautifully against deep blue Siberian squill (*Scilla sibirica*) and striped squill (*Puschkinia scilloides*).

Colchicum

(*kol*-kih-kum)
autumn crocus, meadow saffron

PLANT AT A GLANCE (photo p. 76)

Type: corm
Flowering Time: fall
Height: 15 cm (6 in.)
Soil: fertile, moist, well drained
Light: full sun
When to Plant: late summer to early fall
How to Plant: 10 cm (4 in.) deep, 15 cm (6 in.) apart
Propagation: division, offsets
Poisonous: yes, all parts harmful when ingested; may cause skin
    irritation
Deer/Rodent Resistant: yes
Good for Forcing: no

This autumn-blooming treasure offers prairie gardeners an enthusiastic burst of color in early September when most other plants are beginning to prepare for winter's arrival. Although it is invariably known as autumn crocus, and even looks like an oversized crocus, it isn't really a crocus at all. Instead it merits a genus of its own—*Colchicum*.

Colchicum takes its name from the ancient kingdom of Colchis on the eastern shore of the Black Sea, a site of treachery by the Greek sorceress and priestess Medea and home for sundry poisonous plants, including *Colchicum*. Its extreme toxicity has been well known since ancient Greek times; however, in the fifth century, Byzantine herbalists discovered it could be used to treat rheumatism, arthritis, and gout. The active ingredient in the plant, an alkaloid called colchicine, is still used to treat gout, and researchers are also discovering that it has anti-cancer properties.

Plant breeders, aware that colchicine causes dwarfing in plants and changes to chromosome counts in plant pollen and egg cells, have long used it in the development of new plant cultivars. The beautiful tetraploid iris cultivars and many recent daylily cultivars exist thanks to colchicine.

Portrait
Although some *Colchicum* bloom in spring, prairie gardeners are attracted to the fall-blooming species, which produce lovely blooms in autumn with nary a leaf to be seen, and grassy foliage the following spring with nary a blossom to be seen.

Colchicum autumnale (autumn crocus). *Ken Girard*

Colchicum flowers are showy goblet-shaped beauties, supported above ground on strong, stemlike tubes up to 8 cm (3 in.) long, which are actually part of the flower. Blossoms can be single or double and come in a range of shades from white, to pink, to violet; some also have white throats.

The foliage that appears the following spring can reach a height and spread of 30 cm (12 in.) or more and must be left to ripen naturally until it withers and dies, just like other bulb foliage. Allowance should be made for this habit at planting time.

You can buy *Colchicum* in late summer or early autumn, plant it in early autumn, and if it hasn't already bloomed on the shelf in the garden center (yes, it can bloom from a bare bulb with no soil or water present), it will put on a colorful show that same autumn, within just a few weeks of being planted. It doesn't get much easier than that!

Only a few *Colchicum* species are available at garden centers or through well-known, mail-order catalogues and they are not cheap.

- *Colchicum autumnale* (15 cm, 6 in.), the hardiest and most readily available species, produces as many as six lavender pink flowers per corm. Cultivars include 'Album' (single white), 'Alboplenum' (double white), 'Plenum' (double pale pink), and 'Pleniflorum' (double amethyst violet). It may flop in windy or rainy weather.
- *Colchicum bornmuellerii* (15 cm, 6 in.) bears one to six funnel-shaped, pale to dark purplish pink flowers with brown anthers. It is often confused with *C. speciosum*, which has yellow anthers.
- *Colchicum cilicicum* (10 cm, 4 in.) produces three to twenty-five funnel-shaped, purplish pink flowers that sometimes flush a deeper shade towards the tips.

- *Colchicum speciosum* (18 cm, 7 in.), the showiest species, has one to three goblet-shaped flowers per corm in shades of purple, often with a white zone at the throat. It is more weather resistant than *C. autumnale*.
- *Colchicum* 'Waterlily' (13 cm, 5 in.) produces up to five showy, double pinkish lilac flowers. Blossoms are top heavy and flop over easily, so they look their best when they are supported by neighboring plants.

Where to Grow

Locate *Colchicum* where its lovely flowers are easily seen but where its ripening foliage won't be intrusive. A perfect spot would be among deciduous trees or shrubs, or among leafy perennials in a flower border. They require a "hot spot" for bulbs to mature. Some people naturalize it in the lawn where green grass provides a lush background to these leafless flowers. However, this means they aren't able to mow the naturalized patch of lawn until after the foliage has ripened the following spring.

Perfect Partners

Colchicum looks lovely planted in front of a redleaf rose (*Rosa glauca*), especially one laden with a good supply of rose hips. It also combines well with other plants with interesting foliage, such as geraniums, silver-leaved artemisia, and the dark-leaved coral bells (*Heuchera* spp.). To disguise the fading foliage, interplant *Colchicum* with tall tulips (*Tulipa*) and narcissus; their foliage all disappears at about the same time in spring.

Convallaria
(con-val-*lay*-ree-ah)
lily-of-the-valley

PLANT AT A GLANCE (photo this page)

Type: rhizome
Flowering Time: late spring
Height: 20 cm (8 in.)
Soil: fertile, moist, well drained
Light: part sun to full shade
When to Plant: fall (bare-root rhizomes); spring through fall (container-grown plants)
How to Plant: 2.5 cm (1 in.) deep, 8 to 10 cm (3 to 4 in.) apart

Convallaria majalis (lily-of-the-valley). *Liesbeth Leatherbarrow*

Propagation: division
Poisonous: yes, all parts harmful when ingested
Deer/Rodent Resistant: yes
Good for Forcing: yes

Convallaria majalis, or lily-of-the-valley, is one of those "ordinary" plants that many gardeners take for granted. This hardy groundcover withstands a great deal of neglect, but despite its toughness, its delicate white floral bells seem tailor-made for a fairy wedding, and the fragrance is among the most heavenly of all garden plants.

It derives its botanical name from two Latin words—*convallis* (valley) and *majalis* (month of May). The common name, lily-of-the-valley, is a literal translation of the medieval *Lilium convallium*.

Lily-of-the-valley, or May lily, was deemed a very useful plant in years gone by. According to John Gerard, a sixteenth-century English botanist, if you put blossoms from lily-of-the-valley into a glass, set the glass in an anthill, and covered it for one month, the liquid in the glass could cure the "paine and griefe of the gout." Apparently you could also use this plant to "cure" freckles by rubbing its blossoms over your skin, relieve migraine headaches, treat eye inflammations, and strengthen memory! Sometimes called glovewort, it was also a useful cure for sore and chapped hands.

Despite its reputed medicinal qualities, the plant is, in fact, somewhat poisonous. It does, however, contain substances that are practical for treating heart and stroke patients. These same substances also seem to work wonders when it comes to restoring lost speech.

Lily-of-the-valley is native to the northern hemisphere, inhabiting woodlands and meadows in England, continental Europe, Asia, and eastern North America. It has been a valued garden plant since the sixteenth century, and its fragrant scent has long been prized for perfumes and soaps. In the language of flowers, lily-of-the-valley betokens the return of happiness, a fitting symbol of spring on the prairies.

Some gardeners avoid lily-of-the-valley because of fears it will overrun other plants. In a perfect environment—light shade with moist, fertile soil—it can spread by creeping rhizomes to form a thick groundcover. However, this is sometimes a desirable trait, and it is by no means as aggressive or difficult to eradicate as the dreaded goutweed (*Aegopodium podagraria*). To its credit, lily-of-the-valley will withstand dry shade once established.

Portrait

Lily-of-the-valley grows from rhizomes that send up growing points called pips, from which the leaves and flowers emerge. The leaves are ovate-lance-shaped and stay an attractive dark green until autumn, making lily-of-the-valley a pleasing groundcover throughout the summer. From the fluted leaves emerge racemes of five to twelve waxy, white, bell-shaped flowers with scalloped edges. Each little bell is 0.5 to 1.5 cm (0.25 to 0.5 in.) across and hangs on a tiny stem from one side of the 8 to 10-cm (3 to 4-in.) main flower stalk. The blossoms mature into red berries.

Although there are several cultivars and a pink-flowered variety, the single white-flowered forms are unquestionably the hardiest and most vigorous. 'Fortin's Giant' has larger leaves and more flowers than the species, while 'Flore Pleno' is a double white cultivar. *Convallaria majalis* var. *rosea* has light mauve pink flowers. A few cultivars with green and white or green and yellow variegated leaves are largely unproven in prairie gardens, but they may be worth a try in a sheltered woodland garden: 'Variegata', 'Hardwick Hall', 'Aureovariegata', and 'Albostriata'.

Where to Grow
Lily-of-the-valley is most at home naturalized beneath deciduous trees. It is also a useful groundcover for a shady slope, or may be planted in a partly sunny corner of a rock garden. The creeping rhizomes and its tendency to spread make it unsuitable for a small perennial border.

Perfect Partners
Plant lily-of-the-valley with an assortment of early to late spring-flowering bulbs that will be happy in part or light shade in summer, including Siberian squill (*Scilla sibirica*), striped squill (*Puschkinia scilloides*), glory-of-the-snow (*Chionodoxa forbesii*), snowdrops (*Galanthus* spp.), and grape hyacinth (*Muscari* spp.). Its leaves are particularly effective in hiding the dying foliage of small bulbs. Shade-loving plants such as hostas, astilbe, bergenia, bleeding heart (*Dicentra* spp.), and Solomon's seal (*Polygonatum* spp.) are all fine companions, as is the lovely 'Annabelle' hydrangea (*Hydrangea arborescens* 'Annabelle').

Corydalis
(ko-*ry*-dah-lis or *ko*-ry-dah-lis)
tuberous corydalis, fumewort

PLANT AT A GLANCE (photo p. 80)

Type: tuber
Flowering Time: mid-spring
Height: 10 to 15 cm (4 to 6 in.)
Soil: fertile, well drained (*Corydalis solida*); fertile, moist, well drained (*C. cava*)

Light: full sun to light shade (*Corydalis solida*); part sun to light shade (*C. cava*)
When to Plant: fall
How to Plant: 5 to 8 cm (2 to 3 in.) deep; 10 to 15 cm (4 to 6 in.) apart
Propagation: division, seed (also self-seeds)
Poisonous: no
Deer/Rodent Resistant: yes
Good for Forcing: no

Most corydalis, including the popular yellow-flowered *Corydalis lutea*, grow from fibrous root stock, although a few early bloomers grow from tubers and are worth including in the early spring lineup. Native to northern Europe, both *C. solida* and *C. cava* are tuberous-rooted woodland plants that develop small spikes of rosy plum, tubular flowers and thrive in dappled shade. They are a bit more difficult to obtain and grow than *C. lutea*, but that shouldn't stop adventuresome gardeners and plant collectors from giving them a try.

Corydalis solida (bulbous corydalis). *Lesley Reynolds*

All corydalis flowers are spurred, or at least come to a spurlike point, so they take their botanic name from the Greek word for lark, a family of birds distinguished by sharp, elongated hind toenails that look like spurs. Corydalis is also sometimes referred to by the rather unlovely names of fumitory, fume-root, or fumewort, so designated because of the slightly smoky smell that results from crushing its roots.

Portrait

Low-growing tuberous corydalis produces short spikes of up to twenty spurred, tubular flowers above finely divided, blue-green, fernlike foliage, giving the soft look of ferns in the garden with the bonus of rosy plum flowers in early spring. Individual plants can form clumps 15 to 25 cm (6 to 10 in.) across that invariably go dormant in summer. The soil must be kept moist, even during dormancy; otherwise, the tubers will dry out.

As its name suggests, *Corydalis solida* grows from a solid tuber, whereas *C. cava* grows from a hollow tuber with a hollow stem base. *C. solida* tubers increase rapidly, sometimes doubling in number each year. *C. cava* spreads much more slowly and is more inclined to self-seed than *C. solida*.

- *Corydalis cava* (syn. *C. bulbosa*) (20 cm, 8 in.) has masses of two-lipped, rosy plum flowers with long spurs held on erect stems above ferny blue-green foliage. 'Alba' is a white form with dark purple bracts.
- *Corydalis solida* (25 cm, 10 in.), fumewort, produces rosy plum, long-spurred flowers on erect stems above ferny blue-green foliage. Named cultivars include 'Beth Evans' (pale pink), 'Blue Dream' (blue), 'George Baker' (coral red), 'Harkov' (bluish violet), Penza Strain (wide range of colors from white to blue, pink, peaches, and reds).

Where to Grow
Both *Corydalis solida* and *C. cava* are naturals for the woodland garden or a partly shaded mixed border. Plant these small corydalis under deciduous trees or shrubs, along pathways, or on the shores of a pond. They are also perfect inhabitants of lightly shaded rock gardens where they make a modest impact spreading among rocks or growing from shallow crevices.

Perfect Partners
Tuberous corydalis foliage and flowers only last a short while in the early spring garden before going dormant, so group them with other small bulbs that bloom at the same time to show them to advantage. Snowdrops (*Galanthus nivalis*), anemones (*Anemone blanda*), squill (*Scilla*), striped squill (*Puschkinia scilloides*), and crocus are all good choices.

Crocus
(*kro*-kus)
crocus

PLANT AT A GLANCE
(photos p. 8, this page)

Type: corm
Flowering Time: early spring
Height: 8 to 15 cm (3 to 6 in.)
Soil: average, well drained
Light: full sun (flowers will not open properly in part sun or shade)

Crocus vernus 'Striped Beauty'. *Liesbeth Leatherbarrow*

When to Plant: spring-blooming in fall, fall-blooming in late summer to early fall; plant immediately after purchase as they start rooting quite early
How to Plant: 5 to 8 cm (2 to 3 in.) deep, 5 to 8 cm (2 to 3 in.) apart
Propagation: division
Poisonous: no
Deer/Rodent Resistant: no
Good for Forcing: yes, Crocus vernus is best

An essential component of the spring garden, crocuses are splendid garden additions, heralding the arrival of spring with chalice-shaped flowers that hug the ground amid grassy foliage. They come in an assortment of sizes, colors, and bloom times, expanding readily to form cheerful colonies wherever they are planted. Among the first spring-flowering bulbs to bloom, familiar crocuses usually put on a show in April and May. However, some fall-blooming crocus species are also hardy on the prairies, lending a splash of color to gardens that are otherwise beginning to fade.

The genus name *Crocus* derives from *krokos*, the Greek word for saffron. Indeed, the source of this prized spice, *Crocus sativus*, is the oldest cultivated species, mentioned in the Song of Solomon, written over three thousand years ago, and portrayed in Minoan paintings dating from 1600 BC. In addition to its culinary value, saffron has also been used in perfumes, as medicine, and to perform magic in religious ceremonies.

Many legends account for the creation of the diminutive crocus. According to Greek mythology, Mercury accidentally killed Europa's son Crocus, and the well-known flowers sprang from the spilled blood of the child. Another legend describes a youth named Crocus who was transformed by the goddess Flora into the flower that bears his name to relieve the agony of his unrequited love.

Portrait
The lovely goblet-shaped crocus blossoms that emerge from the ground, apparently stemless (although the true stem resides underground), come in every imaginable shade of white, yellow, and purple; many are marked with contrasting colors. Their full beauty can only be appreciated on sunny days, because the flowers remain tightly closed on dull days and at night. Crocus foliage is grasslike and characterized by a silvery white midrib.

The most familiar and vigorous crocus for prairie gardens is *Crocus vernus*, or Dutch crocus, always available in local garden centers at summer's end. However, gardeners should not overlook the value of other crocus species, such as *C. chrysanthus* and *C. tommasinianus*. Although they usually have smaller blossoms than *C. vernus*, species crocus bloom earlier, thus extending the crocus bloom season, and often produce more flowers per corm, making them better candidates for naturalizing. Species crocus are a little harder to come by than *C. vernus*, but many are available through mail-order catalogues and are worth the search.

Crocuses that have spent a few seasons in the ground usually bloom earlier than those of the same variety planted the previous season.

- *Crocus ancyrensis* 'Golden Bunch' (5 cm, 2 in.), Ankara crocus, produces clusters of scented, richly colored orange-yellow flowers in clusters of five. It is extremely early blooming.
- *Crocus chrysanthus* (8 cm, 3 in.), snow crocus, produces fragrant, cupped flowers in shades of cream to deep golden yellow, often suffused or veined in bronze on the outside. A number of named varieties and hybrids are available, including 'Blue Bird' (pale blue with purple marks on outside), 'Blue Pearl' (white with lilac on outside), 'Cream Beauty' (cream with greenish base and golden yellow throat), 'E. A. Bowles' (yellow with purple marks on outside), 'Eye-catcher' (pale gray with purple on outside), 'Ladykiller' (white with deep violet marks on outside), and 'Snow Bunting' (white).
- *Crocus speciosus* (15 cm, 6 in.) blooms in the fall, producing solitary violet blue flowers veined with dark blue before the foliage appears. Two attractive cultivars are 'Oxonian' (deep mauve), and 'Conqueror' (sky blue).
- *Crocus tommasinianus* (10 cm, 4 in.) has slender, long flowers and dark green leaves with a white stripe. Named cultivars include 'Barr's Purple' (purple with silver on the outside), 'Ruby Giant' (red-purple), and 'Whitewell Purple' (red-purple on the outside and pale silvery purple inside). *C. tommasinianus* f. *albus* is a pure white form.
- *Crocus vernus* (13 cm, 5 in.), Dutch crocus, has white or lilac purple, cup-shaped flowers and white-striped leaves. Named varieties include 'Pickwick' (white striped with lilac), 'Purpureus Grandiflorus' (violet), 'Queen of the Blues' (lilac blue), 'Remembrance' (violet), 'Sky Blue' (blue), 'Striped Beauty' (silver gray with mauve stripes and purple bases), and 'Yellow Mammoth' (the biggest yellow-flowering selection).

Where to Grow

Plant crocuses in rock gardens, beside paths, or even in large gaps between stones in pathways. They are enchanting in perennial beds or under deciduous trees, and may also be naturalized in turf or tucked in amidst low-growing groundcovers. As with all small bulbs, the best effect is achieved by mass planting.

Perfect Partners

Combine crocuses with plantings of delightful early spring bulbs, such as deep blue Siberian squill (*Scilla sibirica*), striped squill (*Puschkinia scilloides*), snowdrops (*Galanthus* spp.), and pink and blue glory-of-the-snow (*Chionodoxa luciliae*). The rich-looking royal purple *Iris reticulata* and *I. histriodes* are other tiny plants that bloom at the same time as many crocus species and cultivars.

Fritillaria
(fri-ti-*lay*-ree-yah)
fritillary

PLANT AT A GLANCE (photos pp. 52, 85)

Type: true bulb
Flowering Time: late spring to early summer
Height: 15 to 45 cm (6 to 18 in.)
Soil: fertile, moist, well drained (*Fritillaria meleagris, F. pallidiflora*); fertile, well drained (*F. michailovskyi, F. pudica*)
Light: full sun (*Fritillaria michailovskyi, F. pudica*); full sun to light shade (*F. meleagris, F. pallidiflora*)
When to Plant: fall
How to Plant: 13 cm (5 in.) deep, 10 cm (4 in.) apart; the fragile, fleshy bulbs with scales should not be allowed to dry out, plant immediately after purchase
Propagation: division, offsets, seed
Poisonous: no
Deer/Rodent Resistant: yes
Good for Forcing: yes, *Fritillaria meleagris* is best

The genus *Fritillaria* attracts plenty of attention from serious bulb collectors for its unusual floral forms, colors, and patterns. Native to Europe, Asia, North Africa, and North America, over one hundred species of fritillaries are found in a wide range of habitats from woodland to alpine screes.

The genus was named by sixteenth-century botanist Matthias de L'Obel, from the Latin *fritillus* (dice box), in reference to the square shape and checkered pattern characteristic of many species. *Fritillaria meleagris*, in cultivation since the sixteenth century, has accumulated an impressive list of intriguing common names: guinea hen flower, snake's head fritillary, checkered lily, the sullen lady, and leper's bell, a reference to the small bells worn by lepers to warn of their approach. The species name *meleagris* is from the Greek word for guinea fowl, since the markings on the flower were thought to resemble the spotted feathers of that bird.

Prairie gardeners can choose from several lovely small fritillary species that are sure to be conversation pieces in any garden. Unfortunately, the granddaddy of the bunch, the impressive *Fritillaria imperialis*, or crown imperial, can't handle our climate.

Fritillaria pallidiflora (Siberian fritillary). *Llyn Strelau*

Portrait

All prairie-hardy fritillary species have bell-shaped blooms that hang down from the top of straight, upright stems. The medium to gray-green foliage is narrowly to broadly lance-shaped and dies back after flowering. Fritillaries grow from fragile lilylike bulbs composed of two or more fleshy scales. Handle these bulbs carefully, and do not allow them to dry out.

The cultivation requirements of fritillary species vary, depending on their native habitat. *Fritillaria meleagris* and *F. pallidiflora* do well in a variety of conditions, ranging from full sun to light shade. However, neither thrives in very hot or dry locations. *F. michailovskyi* and *F. pudica* prefer full sun and dislike excessive moisture, especially during dormancy, so are good choices for sunny, dry gardens.

- *Fritillaria camschatcensis* (45 cm, 18 in.), black sarana, produces intriguing dark black-purple, sometimes yellow or green, clusters of bell-shaped flowers and glossy, light green foliage.
- *Fritillaria meleagris* (45 cm, 18 in.), checkered lily, is the most readily available species. The blooms, usually single and shaped like square bells, are checkered in shades of reddish purple and pink and are up to 4 cm (1.5 in.) long. (This European species is much beloved by *Canis cambricus*, the Welsh terrier). *F. meleagris* f. *alba* is a white form. Named varieties may be difficult to obtain, but are worth the hunt. Look for 'Adonis' (creamy white checkered with pale purple), 'Aphrodite' (pure white), 'Artemis' (purple checkered with green), 'Charon' (dark purple checkered with black), and 'Saturnis' (red-violet). In addition, mixed varieties are sometimes available. Checkered lilies may be short lived.
- *Fritillaria michailovskyi* (20 cm, 8 in.) bears deep reddish

purple, squarish bell-shaped flowers with flared yellow tips. Each stem carries umbels of one to four flowers that are up to 3 cm (1.25 in.) long. This delightful little bulb was discovered in northern Turkey in 1905, but only brought into cultivation in 1965.

- *Fritillaria pallidiflora* (45 cm, 18 in.), Siberian fritillary, produces six or more cream to greenish yellow, squarish bell-shaped flowers with faint brown checkers, measuring up to 4 cm (1.5 in.) in length. Although its flowers are delightful in appearance, some people find their scent unpleasant.
- *Fritillaria pudica* (15 cm, 6 in.), yellow fritillary, has pure yellow flowers that darken to copper red as they age. The cone-shaped blooms are 2.5 cm (1 in.) long, and there are usually one or two flowers per stem. This very hardy little plant is a western North American native found in British Columbia, down the eastern slopes of the Cascades to California and east to Utah, and in Wyoming, Montana, North Dakota, and Alberta.

Where to Grow

Fritillaria meleagris and *F. pallidiflora* are striking near the front of a border or along a path in a partly shaded woodland garden. *F. meleagris* is also ideal for naturalizing with native or ornamental grasses, although it is too large and late blooming for lawn naturalization. Sunny rock gardens are perfect locations for *F. michailovskyi* and *F. pudica*, which appreciate good drainage and dry summer conditions.

Perfect Partners

The dangling bells of fritillaries are charming suspended above spiky blue grape hyacinth (*Muscari* spp.), which blooms at about the same time. In the border, the purple-checkered flowers of *Fritillaria meleagris* show up beautifully against the velvety green leaves of lady's mantle (*Alchemilla mollis*). In partly shaded areas, combine fritillaries with ajuga, primulas, violas, blue-eyed Mary (*Omphalodes verna*), and mound-forming plants such as astilbe, dwarf goatsbeard (*Aruncus aethusifolius*), or foamflower (*Tiarella* spp.) that will fill in once the foliage dies back. Rock garden fritillaries are lovely displayed against low-growing companions such as creeping veronica (*Veronica pectinata*, *V. prostrata*), perennial candytuft (*Iberis sempervirens*), and white-flowered rock cress (*Arabis caucasica* 'Snowball').

Galanthus

(gal-*an*-thus)
snowdrop

PLANT AT A GLANCE (photos pp. 37, 88)

Type: true bulb
Flowering Time: early spring
Height: 10 to 15 cm (4 to 6 in.)
Soil: fertile, moist, well drained
Light: full to part sun
When to Plant: early fall
How to Plant: 8 to 10 cm (3 to 4 in.) deep, 5 to 8 cm (2 to 3 in.) apart
Propagation: division, offsets, seed (also self-seeds)
Poisonous: yes, bulbs harmful when ingested, may cause skin
   irritation
Deer/Rodent Resistant: yes
Good for Forcing: yes

An early bloomer on the prairies, the tiny snowdrop is one of the first flowers to venture forth in spring. Its nodding, ivory-white flowers with interesting green markings and brilliant jade green foliage are a welcome sight as winter fades and spring begins to flourish. The snowdrop's delicate beauty belies its true nature; it's actually a tough little customer, easily surviving several degrees of frost and those inevitable heavy, prairie spring snowfalls.

The snowdrop, still frequently found in old English monastery gardens, was likely introduced into England by fifteenth-century Italian monks who recognized its value for healing wounds. Because it was also usually blooming in England by the beginning of February, the snowdrop became associated with Candlemas Day (February 2), a Christian religious celebration observing the Purification of the Virgin. This association gave rise to many common names for this little bulb, among them Candlemas bells, purification flower, Mary's tapers, and procession flower. Other attractive names such as February fair-maids, snow bells, and snow piercers allude to its habit of flowering very early, sometimes even before the snow has melted.

The genus name *Galanthus* is an apt one; it derives from two Greek words, *gala* (milk) and *anthos* (flower), which translates as milk flower and refers to the ivory white color of its blossoms.

Of the almost two dozen species of snowdrops from around the world, two are readily available to prairie gardeners—*Galanthus nivalis* and the larger *G. elwesii*. However, if you should come across others in your travels, such as *G. gracilis*, *G. ikariae*, *G. plicatus*, and *G. rizehensis*, give them a try. They differ either in size or in the character of the green markings on the petals, making them great collectibles.

Make sure that the snowdrop bulbs you buy were propagated in commercial nurseries. Snowdrops have been over collected in the wild, so many *Galanthus* species are on the endangered list.

Portrait

Hardy snowdrops are distinguished by two, sometimes three, narrow, strappy blue-green leaves, each with a hard, white tip. A short, arching stem, reaching just beyond the leaves, supports a single, nodding blossom that consists of six tepals (petals and sepals)—three large ones on the outside and three smaller ones inside, clasped together by a small green cap, similar to the vasecap of a lamp. The milky white flowers of almost all snowdrops resemble drop-shaped necklace pendants (hence, the common name snowdrop) and have characteristic green markings whose shape, number, and position vary with the species. Some are also lightly scented, although this is usually more apparent indoors than out. Snowdrop foliage ripens quickly, so is never really an eyesore in the garden.

Galanthus nivalis (snowdrop). *Liesbeth Leatherbarrow*

The common snowdrop (*Galanthus nivalis*) sports a pair of leaves from 5 to 15 cm (2 to 6 in.) long, and a blossom 2 cm (0.75 in.) long. Blossoms have inner tepals, each with an inverted, V-shaped green marking at its tip. Two plump, multi-petaled, double cultivars, 'Flore Pleno' and 'Plenus', are often available, as is the taller 'Samuel Arnott', which grows to 20 cm (8 in.) in height and has beautiful nodding 3-cm (1.25-in.) long blossoms.

As its name implies, the giant snowdrop (*G. elwesii*) is, on average, larger than the common snowdrop. Its sometimes twisted leaves are slightly longer and broader, up to 30 cm (12 in.) long and 3 cm (1.25 in.) across, and its slender, honey-scented blossoms are about 3 cm (1.25 in.) long. Each inner tepal has two green markings, one at the base and one at the tip; interestingly, these sometimes merge to form a green stripe down the tepal's length.

Where to Grow

Snowdrops, which are native to woodland and rocky environments, are perfect for naturalizing under trees and shrubs or in lawns, or for popping into a rock garden. They are equally charming at the front of perennial and mixed borders where they can be readily seen and appreciated. Because their flowers are small, snowdrops are most effective when planted in drifts, large or small. Coincidentally, they also bloom best in crowded conditions, and may be left undisturbed for years. Snowdrop colonies gradually increase in size as the result of self-seeding.

Perfect Partners

Snowdrops usually bloom at the same time as the tiny, gold-flowered winter aconite (*Eranthis hyemalis*) and often overlap in bloom time with *Iris reticulata* and hellebores (*Helleborus*). They also make a fabulous display growing through low groundcovers such as creeping thyme (*Thymus* spp.), phlox, and rock cress (*Arabis* spp.), or nestled at the base of blue-leaved ornamental grasses, such as blue oat grass (*Helictotrichon sempervirens*).

Snowdrop Lore

- Some people believed that a bowl of snowdrops brought into the house on Candlemas Day (February 2) would purify the house and all it contained.
- Others considered it dangerous to pick snowdrops because they populated ancient churchyards and were thus a death omen; the fact that their white blossoms resembled the color of mourning for children also made them perilous goods.
- According to some, it was unwise to pick snowdrops before Valentine's Day if you were planning to get married; if you did, your wedding wouldn't happen that year.
- It was also believed that if the first snowdrop to bloom was picked and brought inside, a family member would be fated to die. This was actually a common belief for all spring-flowering blossoms, including primroses, violets, and daffodils.
- Country folk refrained from bringing snowdrops inside until all their chickens had laid eggs—otherwise, no eggs!

Iris
(*eye*-riss)
iris

PLANT AT A GLANCE (photos pp. 92, 93)

Type: true bulb or rhizome
Flowering Time: early spring to mid-summer, depending on the type
Height: 15 to 100 cm (6 to 40 in.)
Soil: average to fertile, well drained (bearded, crested, and bulbous irises); fertile, moist, well drained (beardless irises)
Light: full to part sun
When to Plant: spring to summer (bearded, crested, and beardless irises); fall (bulbous irises)
How to Plant: plant bearded irises with the tops of the rhizomes slightly exposed and 8 to 45 cm (3 to 18 in.) apart, depending on size; if

planted too deeply, they may rot or not bloom. Beardless and crested iris rhizomes may be planted just beneath the soil surface, 8 to 45 cm (3 to 18 in.) apart, depending on size. Plant small iris bulbs 8 to 10 cm (3 to 4 in.) deep, 5 to 10 cm (2 to 4 in.) apart.

Propagation: division, seed

Poisonous: yes, plant juices and rhizomes harmful when ingested, may cause skin irritation

Deer/Rodent Resistant: no

Good for Forcing: yes, bulbous types only

After the tulips have waned and before the glory of the lilies, many a prairie garden is adorned with clumps of boldly flowering bearded irises, followed by their equally lovely but less flamboyant Siberian cousins. Irises, undoubtedly among the most beautiful and dependable inhabitants of the perennial garden, are a large and diverse genus. There are over three hundred iris species and thousands of cultivars, and although not all of these are suited to prairie growing conditions, there are enough hardy varieties to suit even the most dedicated iris collector.

Irises are native to the temperate regions of the northern hemisphere, and have been cultivated for many centuries. Because the plant comes in almost all colors of the rainbow, it was named after Iris, the swift-footed messenger of the ancient Greek gods. She traversed the rainbow from one end to the other, carrying messages between the gods, and from the gods to mortals. One of Iris's duties was to lead the souls of women to the Elysian Fields, and as a result, the Greeks often placed iris blossoms on the graves of women.

The iris has long been associated with the French monarchy. In the fifth century, the army of King Clovis of France escaped defeat at the hands of the Goths by fording the Rhine River where they noticed yellow iris (probably *Iris pseudacorus*) growing towards its center (indicating shallow water). In gratitude, Clovis declared the iris the symbol of his army's salvation and immediately changed his banner emblem from three toads to three irises.

Iris also figured in the unsuccessful 1147 crusade of Louis VII, who adopted it as his emblem because of a dream. In France the iris became known as *fleur-de-Louis*, then *fleur-de-luce* (flower of light), and eventually *fleur-de-lis* (flower of the lily)—both irises and daffodils were often referred to as lilies in earlier times. The three parts of the *fleur-de-lis* represent faith, wisdom, and valor.

Portrait

The *Iris* genus can be subdivided into several groups with a considerable range of sizes, flower shapes and colors, and cultivation requirements. Most prairie-hardy irises grow from rhizomes, but there are a few enchanting little bulbous irises also worth a try. Hybridized bearded irises often have huge and showy ruffled blooms; beardless or crested irises bear smaller and daintier flowers suitable for informal or naturalized gardens.

- Bearded irises are complex hybrids of many species. The large rhizomes produce fans of broad, sword-shaped leaves above which rise flower stems with multiple blooms. Each bloom is composed of six petals—the three that point upward are called standards, while the three downward-curving petals are called falls. The beard is a fuzzy strip that runs down the center of the falls. Bearded irises are classified according to size and blooming time.
  - *Iris* x *pumila* hybrids include miniature dwarf (20 cm, 8 in.) and standard dwarf (20 to 30 cm, 8 to 12 in.) bearded irises. The miniature dwarf irises are the first to bloom, in mid to late spring, closely followed by the standard dwarf. They are the hardiest and earliest blooming of all the bearded irises. Although there is a wide range of colors, there are fewer named cultivars than for the larger irises. Some good selections for prairie gardens are 'Little Dutch Girl' (violet blue, dark purple beard), 'Little Sapphire' (pale blue), 'Spring Violets' (violet blue), 'Red at Last' (burgundy bronze, gold beard), 'Cherry Garden' (purplish red), 'Ritz' (lemon yellow, copper brown beard), and 'Sarah Taylor' (creamy yellow, blue beard).
- Larger bearded irises are intermediate (40 to 76 cm, 16 to 30 in.), miniature tall (40 to 76 cm, 16 to 30 in.), border (40 to 76 cm, 16 to 30 in.), and tall (76 to 120 cm, 30 to 48 in.). These bloom from early to mid-summer. Tall bearded irises are frequently bred for beauty rather than endurance and are generally less hardy on the prairies than their shorter counterparts. Purchasing plants from prairie iris breeders and growers is a good way to obtain irises that will survive our cold winters.
- *Iris pallida* 'Variegata' (60 cm, 24 in.), sweet iris, is a bearded iris chiefly grown for its striking green and white-striped foliage, although it also boasts pretty lavender blue flowers in early summer. 'Aureo-marginata' has striped gold and green leaves.
- Crested irises (bloom mid-summer) have a crest or ridge on each fall instead of a beard.
  - *Iris cristata* (15 cm, 6 in.) is a delightful woodland iris that prefers dappled shade. Its bluish lilac flowers are marked with a white patch at the base of each petal and an orange

or yellow crest on each fall.
I. cristata f. *alba* is a white-flowered form.

- Beardless irises (bloom from early to mid-summer)
  - *Iris sibirica* (60 to 100 cm, 24 to 40 in.), the elegant Siberian iris, produces enchanting flowers in summer composed of three standards and three falls, but no beard. These irises are valued for their vase-shaped clusters of tall, grassy leaves, which remain green and upright long after

Iris x *pumila* 'Little Sapphire'. *Liesbeth Leatherbarrow*

blooming has ceased, adding pleasing vertical accents to the border. They are untroubled by pests and disease, and require very little maintenance. Most cultivars are in shades of blue and purple, but there are also white, yellow, wine red, and pink selections. Hybridizers have developed over fifteen hundred Siberian iris cultivars, including tetraploid forms that carry twice the usual number of chromosomes and usually bear larger flowers and have more upright foliage than those with a normal complement (diploid). A few cultivars are generally available each spring at garden centers, but if you get hooked on these troublefree beauties, check out specialty iris catalogues that offer a greater selection. Some outstanding performers are 'Butter and Sugar' (70 cm, 28 in.), white and yellow; 'Caesar's Brother' (100 cm, 40 in.), dark violet; 'Chilled Wine' (76 cm, 30 in.), wine red; 'Dreaming Yellow' (75 cm, 30 in.), white and yellow; 'Fourfold White' (80 cm, 32 in.), 15-cm (6-in.) white blooms; 'Ruffled Velvet' (60 cm, 24 in.), velvety purple; 'Silver Edge' (76 cm, 30 in.), sky blue flowers

Bearded *Iris* 'Fresno Frolic'. *Liesbeth Leatherbarrow*

92

marked with yellow and white at the base of the petals and a fine, silver, wirelike edge to each petal; 'Super Ego' (76 cm, 30 in.), light blue; 'Welcome Return' (60 cm, 24 in.), lilac; and 'Wing on Wing' (95 cm, 38 in.), white ruffled.

- Several beardless irises are native to wet areas and are ideal for pond or pondside plantings. *Iris laevigata* (90 cm, 36 in.) has purple-blue, white, or purple and white flowers; there are several named varieties, including a pink cultivar called 'Rose Queen'. *I. pseudacorus* (90 cm, 36 in.), yellow flag iris, has yellow flowers marked with brown or violet. The blooms of *I. versicolor*, blue flag iris, are usually light to dark violet blue. Cultivars include 'Kermesina' (reddish purple), and 'Rosea' (pink). Despite their boggy origins, given adequate moisture all these irises will adapt to life in the perennial border.
- *Iris setosa* (15 to 30 cm, 6 to 12 in.), arctic iris, has blue or purple flowers and is a good choice for rock gardens.
- Spuria irises (120 to 200 cm, 48 to 78 in.) are tall beauties for the iris connoisseur. Several species are hardy in prairie gardens, preferring fertile, well-drained soil that is kept on the dry side during dormancy and full sun. Look for *I. spuria* (purple), *I. spuria* subsp. *musulmanica* (blue or white), *I. orientalis* (white and yellow), and *I. crocea* (yellow).
- Bulbous irises
  - Reticulated irises (10 to 15 cm, 4 to 6 in.), particularly *Iris histrioides* and *I. reticulata*, are the most reliable bulbous irises for the prairies. Often blooming as early as the end of March, they welcome spring with diminutive pale to deep blue, or violet purple flowers. Although the narrow, grassy leaves continue to grow once blooming has finished, they do remain inconspicuous. There are several fine named varieties,

Iris reticulata 'Joyce'. Liesbeth Leatherbarrow

although there is a bit of confusion over which species they belong to. Depending on the source, some of these varieties may be categorized as *I. histrioides*, *I. reticulata*, or as hybrids. Try 'Cantab' (pale blue with orange markings), 'Harmony' (sky blue with yellow markings), 'Joyce' (sky blue with yellow markings), 'J.S. Dijt' (reddish purple with orange markings), 'Katherine Hodgkin' (pale blue marked with fine dark blue lines and yellow markings), and 'Major' (deep blue with white and yellow markings). Slightly less hardy, but worth a try, is *I. danfordiae* (15 cm, 6 in.), with golden yellow flowers freckled with brown.

- Juno irises bloom in mid to late spring. The best choice for prairie gardens is *Iris bucharica* (30 cm, 12 in.), which bears up to six yellow or yellow and white flowers per stem. Make sure to mulch these irises for winter protection.

Where to Grow

Both bearded and beardless irises are staples of the sunny perennial or mixed border where the foliage adds a spiky or grassy texture all summer long. Tall irises should be placed in the middle of the border, while smaller types look best grouped near the front of a border or in a rock garden.

Siberian and other large beardless irises are lovely specimen plants, especially when planted beside a pond or displayed in a large container. Move container-grown irises into the ground for the winter.

Spring-flowering bulbous irises are perfect rock garden bulbs. They are also lovely naturalized under deciduous trees or planted in turf. Because the flowers are small and bloom when little else has emerged, plant them along a frequently traveled pathway or tuck them beneath low-growing groundcovers at the front of a border where they will be visible from indoors.

Perfect Partners

Bearded irises suit perennials that bloom in early summer and offer contrasting foliage texture. Lady's mantle (*Alchemilla mollis*), cranesbill (*Geranium* spp.), coral bells (*Heuchera* spp.), and Oriental poppy (*Papaver orientale*) all fill the bill. In the rock garden, team small bearded irises with fan columbine (*Aquilegia flabellata*), maiden pink (*Dianthus deltoides*), candytuft (*Iberis sempervirens*), and *Primula auricula*.

Siberian and other beardless irises are graceful foils for many hardy perennials. Try them with columbine (*Aquilegia* spp.), artemisia, Oriental poppy (*Papaver orientale*), cranesbill (*Geranium* spp.), roses, peonies (*Paeonia*), veronica, lady's mantle (*Alchemilla mollis*), campanula, and *Sedum* 'Autumn Joy'.

Spring-flowering bulbous irises are enchanting with other early bulbs such as crocus, snowdrops (*Galanthus* spp.), and Siberian and striped squill (*Scilla sibirica, Puschkinia scilloides*).

Liatris
(lee-*ah*-tris)
gayfeather, blazing star

PLANT AT A GLANCE (photos pp. 24, 96)

Type: corm or tuberous root
Flowering Time: late summer
Height: 50 to 150 cm (20 to 60 in.)
Soil: average to fertile, moist, well drained (*Liatris ligulistylis*,
  L. spicata); average to fertile, well drained (*L. aspera, L. punctata,
  L. pycnostachya*)
Light: full to part sun
When to Plant: spring (bare corms and tuberous roots); spring through
  fall (container-grown plants)
How to Plant: 5 cm (2 in.) deep, 10 to 30 cm (4 to 12 in.) apart;
  soak corms or tuberous roots in tepid water overnight before
  planting
Propagation: division, seed
Poisonous: no
Deer/Rodent Resistant: no
Good for Forcing: no

Liatris is a purely North American genus of great versatility and striking
beauty. The fuzzy wands of rosy purple or white flowers attract bees,
butterflies, and florists alike, but nary an insect pest. This hardy plant,
also known as gayfeather, blazing star, snakeroot, and prairie button, is
found both on the western prairies and in open woodlands in eastern
North America.

The fleshy corms of the prairie native *Liatris punctata* were used for
food by Native people, but gardeners paid little attention to the plant
until it became a hit with English gardeners and florists in the nineteenth
century. Today, most prairie gardeners recognize the fine qualities of this
native plant, and agree that the shaggy floral candles of liatris are a stand-
out in the late-summer garden.

Portrait
Liatris produces clumps of linear basal foliage from which arise stiff
bloom stalks clad with shorter leaves. The unusual flower clusters are
arranged along the upper end of the bloom stalk in a dense spike. The
small, purple or white flower heads consist entirely of button-shaped
clusters of seed-producing disk florets; petal-like ray florets are absent.
The flower heads open from the top down, unlike other spiky plants, to
reveal the inner filamentous florets that give liatris its furry look.

Liatris is an extremely well-behaved plant, forming a tidy, upright clump in the garden that does not require frequent division. Staking is not necessary for shorter species, but may be required for taller versions, especially if they are grown in overly rich soil. Because the flower spikes bloom from the top down, they can be deadheaded by trimming spike ends as flowers fade. Since this type of dead-heading will only serve to tidy the plant and won't encourage reblooming, consider leaving the flower stalks intact so that birds can enjoy the seeds during fall and winter.

Several species of liatris are hardy on the prairies, although *Liatris spicata* is the most commonly available.

Liatris ligulistylis (meadow blazing star). *Llyn Strelau*

- *Liatris aspera* (1.5 m, 5 ft.), rough gayfeather, bears lavender purple flowers, each 1.5 cm (0.5 in.) across on 45-cm (18-in.) spikes.
- *Liatris ligulistylis* (60 cm, 24 in.), meadow blazing star, has round, bright purple flower heads up to 3 cm (1.25 in.) across.
- *Liatris punctata* (80 cm, 32 in.), snakeroot or dotted blazing star, produces crowded 30-cm (12-in.) spikes of deep rosy purple flowers. The stiff, narrow leaves are covered with resinous dots, hence, the botanical name *punctata*, meaning spotted.
- *Liatris pycnostachya* (1.5 m, 5 ft.), Kansas gayfeather, produces dense 45-cm (18-in.) spikes of bright purple flower heads, each 1.5 cm (0.5 in.)

Liatris spicata (gayfeather). *Lesley Reynolds*

across. 'Alexander' is a sturdy cultivar with thick spikes of purple flowers; 'Alba' is white.

- *Liatris spicata* (90 cm, 36 in.), spike gayfeather, is the most popular garden species, bearing pink-purple or white flowers 1.5 cm (0.5 in.) across. This species requires more moisture than other species, but is reasonably drought tolerant once established. 'Kobold' (50 cm, 20 in.) is an excellent compact, purple-flowered cultivar; other named varieties are 'Alba' (off white), 'Blue Bird' (blue violet), 'Floristan White' (creamy white), 'Floristan Violet' (lustrous violet), 'Silver Tip' (lavender), and 'Snow Queen' (white).

Where to Grow
All liatris species and cultivars will provide strong vertical lines in a formal perennial border or an informal cottage-style garden. Drought-tolerant *Liatris aspera* and *L. punctata* are ideal plants to sprinkle here and there in a natural prairie garden.

Perfect Partners
Liatris is splendid in the late-summer border with goldenrod (*Solidago* spp.), black-eyed Susan (*Rudbeckia* spp.), prairie coneflower (*Ratibida columnifera*), purple coneflower (*Echinacea purpurea*), monarda, and garden phlox. The bold magenta flowers also combine well with ornamental grasses, artemisia, German statice (*Goniolimon tataricum*), pearly everlasting (*Anaphalis* spp.), globe thistle (*Echinops* spp.), and a variety of sedums.

Lilium
(*lil*-ee-um)
lily

PLANT AT A GLANCE (photos pp. 5, 13, 16, 25, 29, 49, 100, 101)

Type: true bulb
Flowering Time: late spring to fall, depending on the type
Height: 0.6 to 1.8 m (2 to 6 ft.)
Soil: fertile, moist, well drained
Light: full to part sun
When to Plant: fall (bare bulbs); spring through fall (container-grown plants); spring plantings of the less-hardy types overwinter better than fall plantings; can be given a head start indoors in early spring and planted into the garden later in the season
How to Plant: 15 to 20 cm (6 to 8 in.) deep (large bulbs), 10 to 15 cm

Lily Lore

- The lily has often been associated with religious figures, among them, Britomartis, a Minoan goddess; Saint Anthony, the protector of marriages; the Virgin Mary; Venus, the Roman goddess of love; and Juno, the queen of gods and the goddess of marriage. Legend has it that Juno's milk spilled as she was nursing her son Hercules; some of the milk drops remained in the sky where they formed the Milky Way, while others landed on earth where they became lilies.
- The Romans used to cure corns with lily bulb juice, and probably brought them to England for this purpose.
- Lily seeds taken in drink were supposed to cure snakebites.
- White lilies were thought to cure the bite of a mad dog.
- According to Anglo-Saxon folklore, if you offered an expectant mother the choice between a lily and a rose, she would have a boy if she chose the lily, and a girl if she chose the rose.
- Lilies were believed to protect against witchcraft and to bar ghosts from entry into the garden.
- Lilies were (and still are, to some extent) a symbol of purity in marriage.
- The lily is the symbol of majesty, according to the Victorian language of flowers.

(4 to 6 in.) deep (small bulbs), 30 to 45 cm (12 to 18 in.) apart; lilies prefer a cool root run, so plant low-growing perennials and annuals at their feet

Propagation: division, offsets, bulbils in leaf axils (some species), scales, seed

Poisonous: no

Deer/Rodent Resistant: no

Good for Forcing: no

With its classic charm and beauty, the lily is truly one of the most popular plants among prairie gardeners. It would be rare to find a prairie garden without at least one conspicuous cluster of familiar trumpet-shaped lily blossoms, keeping a steady eye on its neighbors in the perennial border.

Lilies have been in cultivation for over five thousand years, from the time of Sumerian civilization in the Tigris-Euphrates Valley. They derive their designation *Lilium* from the Greek *leirion*, the ancient name of the Madonna lily (*L. candidum*), which is one of the oldest known lilies.

Over one hundred lily species are known today, all native to the temperate regions of the northern hemisphere. European and North American species lilies have been grown in gardens for decorative and medicinal purposes for centuries, but it wasn't until 1804 that plant collector William Kerr introduced the first Asiatic species to the West. There followed a lily-collecting frenzy in Asia, which finally petered out in the early twentieth century, at about the same time that plant breeders began a lily-breeding frenzy of their own. Thanks to plant breeders' skills and perseverance, lilies are now available in practically any color (except blue), shape, and size, which means there is a lily to be savored for every conceivable setting in the garden.

Portrait

A phenomenal number of lily hybrids are available to the prairie gardener, in an artist's palette of colors, some bright and hot, others soft and elegant. Lilies produce six-petaled flowers that may be upfacing, outfacing or sidefacing, or downfacing. Flower form varies from bowl- to trumpet- to star-shaped, and many types have recurved petals. The flowers have prominent pollen-laden stamens, attractive to bees and butterflies, and are usually clustered atop sturdy stems clad with medium to dark green, lance-shaped leaves. Very tall lilies may require staking, especially in windy locations.

Conventional wisdom and experience indicate that trumpet, Aurelian, and Oriental lilies are not fully hardy on the prairies. However, more and more prairie gardeners are reporting success with these fragrant beauties, just by providing good winter protection. Experienced growers also find that spring plantings of these lilies are more apt to overwinter in cold areas than fall plantings, especially if they have been given a head start indoors. This group of lilies will likely never be long-lived in our challenging growing conditions, but four or five years of pleasure from their showy, fragrant blossoms is worth the effort, according to those who have tried.

Early-blooming and dependable, Asiatic hybrids are undoubtedly the easiest to grow and obtain. However, new hybrids developed on the prairies are also outstanding choices for both the beginning gardener and the lily connoisseur. Several species, which are both less demanding and less available than the hybrids, are also recommended in the following list.

- *Lilium* x *hybridum* (lily hybrids)
  - Asiatic hybrids (0.6 to 1.5 m, 2 to 5 ft.) produce upfacing, outfacing, or downfacing blossoms in a wide range of colors, including reds, oranges, yellows, pinks, and various combinations, in early to mid-summer. These lilies are not known for their fragrance. A few tried and true favorites include 'Bold Knight' (114 cm, 45 in.), bright red, outfacing; 'China' (76 cm, 30 in.), soft pink, upfacing; 'Connecticut King' (90 cm, 36 in.), copper yellow, upfacing; 'Enchantment' (90 cm, 36 in.), the classic orange-speckled Asiatic lily, upfacing; 'Little Yellow Kiss' (70 cm, 28 in.), double yellow, upfacing; 'Roma' (105 cm, 42 in.), creamy white to yellow, upfacing; 'Sorbet' (120 cm, 48 in.), white with pink-red edges, upfacing; 'Sun Ray' (90 cm, 36 in.), yellow, upfacing; and 'Tiger Babies' (76 cm, 30 in.), peach pink with chocolate spots, downfacing. The short 'Pixie' series Asiatic lilies are perfect choices for growing in containers.
  - Aurelian-trumpet hybrids (90 to 120 cm, 36 to 48 in.), Orientpets, comprise an exciting group of cultivars hybridized from Aurelian trumpet lilies and Oriental lilies at the Morden Research Centre in Manitoba. These fragrant lilies bloom three to five weeks after Asiatic lilies and have proven hardy

in Zone 3 without special winter protection. Cultivars include 'Starburst Sensation' (90 cm, 36 in.), outfacing, bowl-shaped, pink flowers with dark pink throats; 'Northern Carillon' (120 cm, 48 in.), trumpet-shaped, fragrant, pink flowers with dark red throats; 'Northern Sensation' (120 cm, 48 in.), a hardier sister to 'Northern Carillon', a more bowl-shaped

Lilium 'Little Yellow Kiss'. *Lesley Reynolds*

flower and a lighter red throat; and 'Northern Beauty' (90 cm, 36 in.), downfacing, recurved dark red flowers with yellow throats.

- Aurelian-Asiatic hybrids (90 to 120 cm, 36 to 48 in.), the Canadian Belles Series, are another exciting Canadian introduction, with several cultivars that bloom from early to mid-summer. 'Ivory Belles' (90 cm, 36 in.) has ivory, out- to upfacing flowers with a slight yellow blush in the center and a gray-purple exterior. 'Silky Belles' (90 to 120 cm, 36 to 48 in.) has white, outfacing, bowl-type flowers with a greenish hue and grayish purple exterior. 'Fiery Belles' (90 to 120 cm, 36 to 48 in.) has orange, out- and upfacing flowers with flared blooms and a purple-brown exterior. 'Creamy Belles' (90 to 120 cm, 36 to 48 in.) has cream out- and upfacing flowers with dark grayish purple exteriors.

- Longiflorum-Asiatic hybrids (60 to 90 cm, 24 to 36 in.) comprise another prairie-hardy group of lilies that bloom from early to mid-summer. Lovely cultivars in the group include 'Camelot' (60 to 90 cm, 24 to 36 in.), powder pink flowers with a yellow band and tiny spots; 'Hello Dolly' (90 cm, 36 in.), maroon red flowers with a softer red throat; 'Kiss Me Kate' (60 to 90 cm, 24 to 36 in.), coral rose flowers with a gold

Lilium 'China'. *Liesbeth Leatherbarrow*

100

star in the center; 'My Fair Lady' (90 cm, 36 in.), soft shell pink flowers, both inside and out, with a soft yellow throat; and 'Showbiz' (90 cm, 36 in.), strong purplish pink flowers with a light creamy yellow glow in the center.

Lilium x Orientpets 'Starburst Sensation' (Orientpet lily). *Llyn Strelau*

- *Lilium lancifolium* (syn. *L. tigrinum*) (0.6 to 1.5 m, 2 to 5 ft.) tiger lily, one of the easiest lilies to grow, produces nodding, recurved, orange-red blooms with dark purple or black spots in mid-summer. Numerous black bulbils nestle in the leaf axils.
- *Lilium martagon* (75 cm, 30 in.), Turk's cap or martagon lily, is an early-summer bloomer and one of the oldest lilies in cultivation. It has nodding, pinkish purple flowers with dark spots at the center; the petals are rolled back or reflexed to give the classic Turk's cap shape. Martagon blossoms are fragrant, but their scent is unpleasant to most people. Interesting hybrids include 'Amelita' (deep purplish pink with dark purple spots), 'Autumn Color' (yellow with red spots), 'Barnholm' (cream), 'Early Bird' (yellow with maroon spots), 'Mrs. R. O. Backhouse' (yellow, outside slightly flushed magenta rose, red spots), and 'Sweet Betsy' (silver pink with maroon spots). These lilies are shade tolerant.
- *Lilium monadelphum* (0.9 to 1.5 m, 3 to 5 ft.) is a lime-tolerant lily species that produces 10-cm (4-in.), yellow, trumpet-shaped blossoms, flecked and spotted with maroon and purple on the inside, flushed purplish brown on the outside. It blooms in early to mid-summer and tolerates sunnier and drier conditions than most lilies.

Lilium x *martagon* 'Amelita' (martagon lily). *Llyn Strelau*

- *Lilium philadelphicum* (20 to 60 cm, 8 to 24 in.), western red lily or wood lily, blooms in early to mid-summer with orange-red, upfacing flowers, often spotted with maroon. It will grow in dappled shade but is happiest in dry, prairielike conditions. The provincial floral emblem of Saskatchewan, this is one of the most drought-tolerant lily species.

Where to Grow

For a striking display, plant lilies in mixed or perennial borders or between deciduous shrubs. With a wide range of mature heights available in lily cultivars, they can be stars in the front, middle, or back of the border. Short, sturdy container-grown plants look elegant planted in large pots, but must be dug into the garden in the fall to overwinter successfully. Dwarf varieties are excellent additions to both containers and rock gardens.

Martagon lilies are most at home in a woodland setting, in dappled shade, or a partly shaded border.

Perfect Partners

Combine lilies with delphiniums, *Achillea* Galaxy Series, coreopsis, monarda, garden phlox, peach-leaved bellflowers (*Campanula persicifolia*), or Canterbury bells (*Campanula medium*). Roses and lilies are a classic combination, while the fountains of Siberian iris (*Iris sibirica*) and daylily (*Hemerocallis* spp.) foliage disguise lily stems once blooming has finished.

Muscari

(moose-*kah*-ree)
grape hyacinth

PLANT AT A GLANCE (photos pp. 13, 104)

Type: true bulb
Flowering Time: mid-spring
Height: 10 to 20 cm (4 to 8 in.)
Soil: average, well drained
Light: full to part sun
When to Plant: fall
How to Plant: 5 cm (2 in.) deep, 8 cm (3 in.) apart
Propagation: offsets, seed (also self-seeds)
Poisonous: no
Deer/Rodent Resistant: yes
Good for Forcing: yes

As the first flush of small spring-flowering bulbs begins to wane, keep your eyes peeled for grape hyacinth announcing its presence with a bold display of blue. Grape hyacinth is one of the easiest bulbs to grow and is of great value in the spring garden. Although it is relatively small, its interesting flower shape, vibrant color, eagerness to naturalize, hardiness, and economical price make it an obvious choice for prairie spring gardens.

Native to the Mediterranean region and southwestern Asia, *Muscari* derives its genus name from one or all of three related words, each meaning "musky," in reference to the musky fragrance of some species: the Arabic *muskarimi*, Latin *muscus*, and Greek *moschos*.

Portrait

All grape hyacinths consist of an elongated, spiky cluster of nodding, bell-shaped flowers that resembles a Lilliputian bunch of grapes—small in stature, but big when it comes to making an impact. Individual flowers consist of six petals, usually in shades of blue, delicately rimmed with white and fused into a tubular shape that separates and flares at the tips, giving rise to the bell shape. The flower spikes of *Muscari armeniacum* open progressively from the bottom upward, whereas those of *M. latifolium* do the reverse, opening progressively from the top downward. This strategy of blossoms opening gradually instead of all at once is a good survival technique for plants, as it extends their potential season of pollination considerably.

Grape hyacinth foliage usually forms grassy clusters of fleshy, strap-shaped leaves, and ranges in color from medium green to blue-gray green, depending on the species. Sometimes the leaves emerge in the fall and overwinter aboveground, with the flowers appearing the following spring.

- *Muscari armeniacum* (15 to 20 cm, 6 to 8 in.), the most familiar grape hyacinth, produces deep purple-blue flower clusters. Individual petals, rimmed in white at the tip, are fused into a tight bell shape. Several cultivars are available to choose from (if you can find them), including 'Blue Pearl' (dark blue blossoms), 'Blue Spike' (soft blue, double blossoms), 'Cantab' (light blue blossoms), and 'Fantasy Creation' (double-flowering blue blossoms that transform into green as they fade). Of these, 'Blue Spike' is most readily available.
- *Muscari botryoides* (15 to 25 cm, 6 to 10 in.), common grape hyacinth, with its sky blue, bell-shaped flowers, rimmed in white, is not readily available. Instead, it is the white cultivar 'Album' that is popular. The 'Album' flower cluster is loose and narrow.

- *Muscari comosum* (syn. *Leopoldia comosa*) (20 to 25 cm, 8 to 10 in.), tassel or feather hyacinth, has a two-tiered flower spike, consisting of a tuft of sterile blue flowers at the top, and greenish brown flowers lower down. *M. comosum* 'Plumosum' is a curious cultivar whose lavender, feathery-looking flowers are actually a series of highly branched, lavender flower stems.
- *Muscari latifolium* (15 to 25 cm, 6 to 10 in.), one-leaf grape hyacinth, lives up to its name by producing one wide, medium green leaf per bulb. Each flower spike has two tiers of flowers; the upper oblong, urn-shaped blossoms are sterile and violet in color, whereas those lower down on the spike are fertile and a true indigo blue. This grape hyacinth is not quite as hardy as the others.

Muscari armeniacum (grape hyacinth) and *Euphorbia polychroma* (spurge). Liesbeth Leatherbarrow

Where to Grow

Whether planted at the front of perennial, mixed, or shrub borders, or tucked into rock gardens or containers, grape hyacinth looks best arranged in groups or drifts. It is also well suited to naturalizing under deciduous trees and shrubs at the edge of a woodland garden. Some gardeners take advantage of the fact that grape hyacinth is a rapid spreader, and create winding rivers of blue in the garden, with other spring-flowering bulbs, such as Darwin or Triumph tulips, populating their "banks."

Perfect Partners

Bright blue and yellow flowers always make a dazzling combination, so plant grape hyacinth with the yellow flowers of spring—leopard's bane (*Doronicum* spp.), *Euphorbia polychroma*, yellow tulip cultivars, and late-flowering narcissus, to name a few. Grape hyacinth also makes a big statement when paired with resonant orange-flowered avens (*Geum coccineum*) and is equally attractive partnered with white-flowered plants, such as snowdrop anemone (*Anemone sylvestris*) and rock cress (*Arabis* spp.), or planted beneath a birch tree (*Betula* spp.) with its brilliant white bark.

Narcissus

(nar-*siss*-us)
narcissus, daffodil

PLANT AT A GLANCE (photos pp. 28, 57, 59, 107, 108, 109, 132)

Type: true bulb
Flowering Time: early to late spring, depending on the type
Height: 10 to 60 cm (4 to 24 in.)
Soil: fertile, moist, well drained
Light: full sun to light shade
When to Plant: early fall
How to Plant: 8 to 20 cm (3 to 8 in.) deep, depending on bulb size,
    5 to 15 cm (2 to 6 in.) apart; bulbs should be planted by mid-
    September at the latest, as narcissus require a fair amount of
    time to grow roots before the onset of winter
Propagation: division, offsets; don't remove offset until basal plate
    from which roots grow has developed
Poisonous: yes, bulbs harmful when ingested, leaves and flowers
    may cause skin irritation
Deer/Rodent Resistant: yes
Good for Forcing: yes

Few sights are as evocative of spring as a display of cheerful yellow narcissus, also commonly known as daffodils or jonquils. Drifts of shining daffodils have long been associated with English gardens, and were mentioned by Shakespeare over two centuries before Wordsworth penned his famous poem extolling their virtues.

The daffodil is an ancient and storied flower, populating Greek and Roman myth and even found in Egyptian tombs. The genus name *Narcissus* is the classical Greek name of a beautiful youth who was entranced by his own reflection in a pond. Depending on which version of the myth you read, he either pined away gazing at the lovely image or drowned attempting to grasp it. The gods then transformed him into a golden daffodil. The word and the mythological figure may be even more ancient, borrowed by the Greeks from ancient Persia.

There are over fifty species of daffodils native to many different habitats in Europe and North Africa. Although some are found as far north as Great Britain, most are indigenous to Spain, Portugal, and other locations around the Mediterranean. Today there are over twenty-five thousand daffodil cultivars, most developed in Great Britain, but a large number originating from the Netherlands and the United States.

Tips for Growing Daffodils

- Purchase good-quality bulbs that are large and heavy for their type.
- Enrich the soil with compost and peat moss before planting bulbs.
- Plant the bulbs no later than mid-September. They require several weeks to grow roots before the ground freezes.
- Plant the bulbs in a sunny location, but not where they will come up too early in the spring, that is, not next to a south-facing house foundation. Do not plant them where the soil will bake dry in the summer, but avoid wet, low-lying areas.
- Add a thick layer of organic mulch over the bulbs after planting.
- Fertilize lightly during growth and bloom season.
- Deadhead flowers as soon as they begin to fade so no energy is wasted making seeds.
- Leave the foliage intact until it dies back naturally. Don't braid or tie up the leaves as this interferes with food production for the bulb.

Portrait

Daffodils grow from onionlike true bulbs clad in a papery brown tunic. The size of the bulb can range from 6 to 18 cm (2.5 to 7 in.), depending on the species or cultivar. Some large bulbs may have two or three offsets; these double- or triple-nosed bulbs produce more flowers. Early in the spring, daffodils produce flat, strappy foliage from which emerge leafless flower stems. After blooming, the foliage gradually ripens and dies by mid-summer.

Each daffodil flower consists of a corona, called a trumpet or cup depending on its length, and a perianth, which consists of an outer ring of six petal-like segments. Flowers may be single or double with a wide variety of shape and form. With so many species and cultivars, it's not surprising that daffodils come in a myriad of colors, ranging from white through yellow to orange, red, apricot, pink, and even green. The bloom season depends on the type of daffodil, and there are daffodils that bloom in early, mid, and late spring.

Gardeners across the prairies report varying success with daffodils. They have proven to be reliable spring bloomers in many Zone 3 gardens, and are tolerant of the below-freezing temperatures we often experience in a prairie spring. Although they are of borderline hardiness in Zone 2, some gardeners in these areas do grow them year after year.

Prairie gardeners should consider planting miniature daffodils, among the best adapted to our climate. The blossoms of these little beauties often last for several weeks, and like their larger relatives, there are cultivars that bloom from early to late spring. Many miniature daffodils will gradually spread and bloom for years without division. In addition, they withstand windy conditions better than taller daffodils, and their maturing leaves are inconspicuous once blooming has ceased.

Daffodils are divided into twelve divisions, based upon flower form, number of flowers per stem, and origin. All of these divisions are hybrids of garden origin, except the tenth, which comprises species and wild forms. Not all daffodil species or cultivars are hardy to prairie conditions; however, it should be noted that many have not yet been extensively tested in our climate. Hopefully, further experimentation by adventurous gardeners will expand the list of prairie-hardy daffodils. Except where otherwise noted, the daffodils listed below should tolerate temperatures down to -40° C (-40° F).

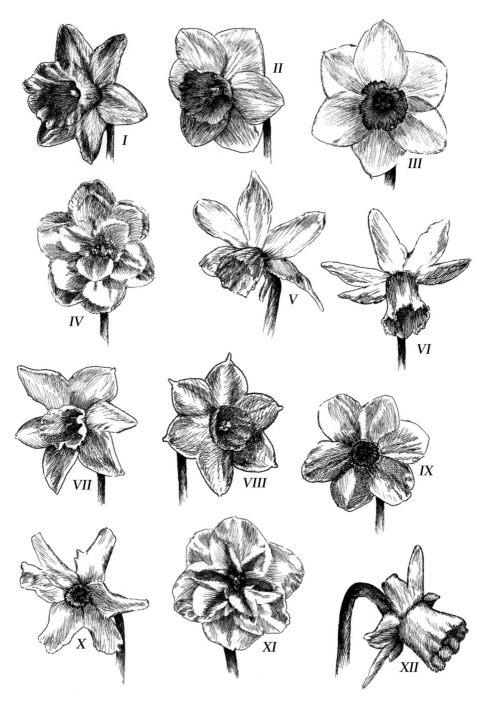

NARCISSUS CLASSIFICATIONS I. Trumpet cultivars: 'Dutch Master' II. Large-or Long-cupped cultivars: 'Salomé' III. Small- or Short-cupped cultivars: 'Merlin' IV. Double cultivars: 'Tahiti' V. Triandrus cultivars: 'Thalia' VI. Cyclamineus cultivars: 'February Gold' VII. Jonquilla cultivars: 'Pipit' VIII. Tazetta cultivars: 'Minnow' IX. Poeticus cultivars: 'Actaea' X. Species and wild forms: *Narcissus poeticus* var. *recurvus* XI. Split-corona cultivars: 'Broadway Star' XII. Miscellaneous: 'Tête à Tête'

- **Division I:** Trumpet cultivars (15 to 60 cm, 6 to 24 in.) have one flower per stem and the trumpet (corona) is as long as or longer than the perianth segments. This is the classic early- to mid-spring blooming, yellow trumpet daffodil typified by 'King Alfred', which was originally introduced in 1899. There are very few authentic 'King Alfred' daffodils around today, but many that may be

Narcissus 'Golden Trumpet'. *Lesley Reynolds*

described as 'King Alfred' types. The 'King Alfred' type daffodils are hardier than the original 'King Alfred'. Superb all-yellow daffodils include 'Dutch Master', 'Golden Harvest', 'Golden Trumpet', 'Unsurpassable', and 'Arctic Gold'. Other cultivars vary in color: 'Spellbinder' (sulphur yellow, trumpet fading to white), 'Trousseau' (white perianth, soft yellow trumpet), and 'Mount Hood' (white perianth, creamy yellow trumpet fading to white).

- **Division II:** Large- or Long-cupped cultivars (20 to 60 cm, 8 to 24 in.) have one flower per stem; the length of the cup (corona) is more than one-third of, but less than the entire length of, the perianth. Try 'Accent' (white perianth, pink cup), 'Ambergate' (coppery orange perianth, red cup), 'Carlton' (fragrant, yellow), 'Ceylon' (golden yellow perianth, orange cup), 'Flower Record' (white perianth, red-rimmed yellow cup), 'Fortune' (yellow perianth, orange cup), 'Ice Follies' (creamy white perianth, frilled, pale

Narcissus 'Rip van Winkle'. *Lesley Reynolds*

yellow cup), and 'Salomé' (creamy white perianth, yellow apricot cup maturing to soft pink).

- **Division III:** Small- or Short-cupped cultivars (15 to 45 cm, 6 to 18 in.) have one flower per stem; the cup or corona is not more than one-third of the length of the perianth. Suggested cultivars are 'Barrett Browning' (white perianth, orange-red cup), 'Merlin' (white perianth, red-rimmed yellow cup), and 'Verona' (white).

Narcissus 'Dove Wings'. *Liesbeth Leatherbarrow*

- **Division IV:** Double cultivars (15 to 45 cm, 6 to 18 in.) sometimes have more than one flower per stem. They may have double perianth segments, double corona, or both, and many are fragrant. The heavy flowers are easily damaged by wind, snow, or rain, so should be planted in a sheltered location. Try 'Cheerfulness' (fragrant, multiflowered, creamy white with yellow centers), 'Rip van Winkle' (syn. *Narcissus minor* subsp. *pumilus* 'Plenus', *N. pumilus* 'Plenus') (bright yellow miniature), 'Sir Winston Churchill' (fragrant, multiflowered, creamy white with orange centers), 'Tahiti' (one large flower per stem, yellow with orange centers), and 'Yellow Cheerfulness' (fragrant, multiflowered, golden yellow).

- **Division V:** Triandrus cultivars (15 to 40 cm, 6 to 16 in.) have two or three nodding, fragrant flowers per stem, often with reflexed perianth segments. Look for 'Hawera' (pale yellow miniature), 'Liberty Bells' (lemon yellow), 'Thalia' (white), and 'Tresamble' (white).

- **Division VI:** Cyclamineus cultivars (15 to 30 cm, 6 to 12 in.) have long trumpets and swept-back

Miniature *Narcissus* 'Tête à Tête'. *Lesley Reynolds*

petals that resemble the parent species *Narcissus cyclamineus.*
Try 'February Gold' (golden yellow perianth, yellow orange
trumpet), 'Dove Wings' (white perianth, lemon yellow cup),
'Jack Snipe' (white perianth, lemon yellow cup), and 'Peeping
Tom' (all yellow).

- **Division VII:** Jonquilla cultivars (15 to 30 cm, 6 to 12 in.) bear
  one to five fragrant, short-cupped flowers per rounded stem.
  Worthy cultivars include 'Bell Song' (ivory white perianth, pink
  cup), 'Pipit' (lemon yellow, cup fading to cream), 'Quail' (golden
  yellow), 'Sweetness' (golden yellow), 'Stratosphere' (golden
  yellow perianth, deep gold cup), and 'Sugarbush' (white perianth, white-edged yellow cup), 'Trevithian' (soft yellow).
- **Division VIII:** Tazetta cultivars (15 to 45 cm, 6 to 18 in.) have
  up to twenty small, fragrant flowers, or three or four large
  ones per stem. This group is not hardy enough for outdoor
  planting on the prairies, but many cultivars are ideal for
  indoor forcing, such as *N. papyraceus,* commonly called
  paperwhite narcissus. Other tazettas that are particularly easy
  to force are sold under the name "paperwhites." These include
  'Grand Soleil d'Or' and 'Ziva'. Poetaz daffodils
  (Tazetta/Poeticus hybrids) are hardier, but few are available.
  'Minnow' (creamy yellow perianth, deep yellow cup, miniature) is a good choice.
- **Division IX:** Poeticus cultivars (30 to 45 cm, 12 to 18 in.) have
  spicily fragrant flowers with large white perianth segments and
  small, red-rimmed, yellow or green cups. There is usually one
  flower per stem. Look for 'Actaea' (white perianth, yellow cup
  edged with dark red), 'Cantabile' (white perianth, green and
  yellow cup edged with red), and 'Milan' (white perianth, green
  and yellow cup edged with red).
- **Division X:** Species and wild forms are of variable hardiness
  and require further testing on the prairies. However, one good
  bet is *Narcissus poeticus* var. *recurvus* (35 cm, 14 in.) old
  pheasant's eye, a fragrant daffodil with recurved, white perianth segments and a red-rimmed yellow cup. Species of
  borderline hardiness are *Narcissus bulbocodium,* *N.*
  cyclamineus, N. minor, N. pseudonarcissus, and *N. triandrus.*
  Because these species often require specialized growing conditions, gardeners should consult a book that offers detailed
  information on narcissus culture. In addition, make sure you
  are buying bulbs that have been propagated in nurseries, not
  collected from the wild.
- **Division XI:** Split-corona cultivars (30 to 45 cm, 12 to 18 in.),
  butterfly daffodils, have coronas split to at least one-third of

their length, which usually spread outward against the large perianth segments. Try 'Broadway Star' (white perianth, white corona segments streaked with orange), 'Cassata' (white perianth, yellow corona segments that mature to white), 'Orangery' (white perianth, orange corona segments), and 'Pearlax' (white perianth, pink corona segments).

- **Division XII:** Miscellaneous daffodils that do not fit into any other division are grouped under this heading. 'Tête à Tête' (golden yellow perianth, yellow orange cup) and 'Jumblie' (golden yellow reflexed perianth, yellow orange cup) are lovely miniature daffodils from this group.

Where to Plant

Daffodils are at their best planted in casual clumps in the middle of informal perennial borders. They may also be naturalized beneath deciduous trees, where they will receive plenty of spring sunshine, or in grassy meadows that will not require mowing until after midsummer. Miniature daffodils are excellent choices for planting in rock gardens.

Perfect Partners

Daffodils are delightful accompanied by dainty small bulbs, such as crocuses, *Iris reticulata*, Siberian squill (*Scilla sibirica*), striped squill (*Puschkinia scilloides*), grape hyacinth (*Muscari* spp.), and glory-of-the-snow (*Chionodoxa* spp.). Group early- to late-blooming varieties of daffodils with species and later-blooming tulips for a fabulous display from April until June. In a lightly shaded garden, plant daffodils with pansies (*Viola* x *wittrockiana*), violets (*Viola*), primulas, and shooting stars (*Dodecatheon meadia*). Suitable rock garden companions for miniature daffodils include rock cress (*Arabis* spp.), false rock cress (*Aubrieta deltoidea*), draba, and moss phlox (*Phlox subulata*).

Daffodil Bloom Sequence

Daffodils are categorized according to when they usually start blooming. Bloom time may extend over two periods, that is, early to mid-spring, or mid to late spring, and will vary according to where the bulbs are planted and the weather from year to year.

Early Spring
- 'Arctic Gold', 'Carlton', 'Ceylon', 'Dove Wings', 'Dutch Master', 'February Gold', 'Fortune', 'Golden Harvest', 'Golden Trumpet', 'Jack Snipe', 'Jumblie', 'Orangery', 'Peeping Tom', 'Spellbinder', 'Tête à Tête', 'Trevithian', 'Trousseau', 'Unsurpassable'

Mid-spring
- 'Accent', 'Ambergate', 'Barrett Browning', 'Broadway Star', 'Cassata', 'Cheerfulness', 'Flower Record', 'Ice Follies', 'Liberty Bells', 'Merlin', 'Minnow', 'Mount Hood', 'Pearlax', 'Pipit', 'Quail', 'Rip van Winkle', 'Sir Winston Churchill', 'Sweetness', 'Sugarbush', 'Tahiti', 'Thalia', 'Tresamble', 'Verona', 'Yellow Cheerfulness'

Late Spring
- 'Actaea', 'Bell Song', 'Cantabile', 'Hawera', 'Milan', *Narcissus poeticus* var. *recurvus*, 'Salomé', 'Stratosphere'

Nectaroscordum
(neck-tar-oh-*skor*-dum)
nectaroscordum

PLANT AT A GLANCE (photo this page)

Type: true bulb
Flowering Time: late spring
Height: 90 to 120 cm (36 to 48 in.)
Soil: fertile, moist, well drained
Light: full to part sun
When to Plant: fall
How to Plant: 10 to 15 cm (4 to 6 in.) deep, 30 cm (12 in.) apart
Propagation: division, bulbils, seed (also self-seeds)
Poisonous: no
Deer/Rodent Resistant: yes
Good for Forcing: no

A garlic-scented drink of the gods? That's the literal translation of *Nectaroscordum*, the genus name of this tall elegant onionlike ornamental plant; however, something like "nectar-bearing onion" is probably closer to the intended meaning of the name. Once considered to be part of the *Allium* genus, and still frequently listed with the alliums in mail-order catalogues, *Nectaroscordum* now defines a genus of its own. Regardless of how it is classified, its pendant clusters of dainty, bell-shaped flowers atop tall, arching stems that swing in the breeze make it an admirable addition to perennial and mixed borders.

Portrait
Two similar members of the genus *Nectaroscordum*—*N. siculum* and *N. s.* subsp. *bulgaricum*—are commonly available in garden centers or mail-order catalogues and they are often mistaken one for the other. Both are very attractive to bees.

Nectaroscordum siculum subsp. *bulgaricum* (nectaroscordum). *Lesley Reynolds*

The blue-green foliage of both plants has a strong, identifiable scent of garlic when bruised or crushed, a reminder of their close relationship with members of the *Allium* genus. The clusters of down-facing, bell-shaped flowers emerge from papery sheaths in late spring atop tall, naked stems that may require staking; then, after blooming, they transform into attractive upright seed heads. These seed heads pose a dilemma to gardeners. On the one hand, they remain attractive in the garden all winter long and are a potential source of food for the local bird population. On the other hand, every seed that spills from the pod onto the ground can and will germinate, leaving gardeners with a big clean-up job the following spring. For those who don't wish to spend their time weeding vast patches of nectaroscordum seedlings, conscientious deadheading is definitely the way to go.

- *Nectaroscordum siculum* (syn. *Allium siculum*) (1.2 m, 4 ft.) produces loose umbels of twenty to thirty white or cream, open bell-shaped flowers, flushed pink with a tinge of pale green at the base; the blue-green foliage is linear, 30 to 40 cm (12 to 16 in.) long.
- *Nectaroscordum siculum* subsp. *bulgaricum* (syn. *N. dioscoridis*, *Allium bulgaricum*) (90 cm, 36 in.) has tall, pagoda-like spires topped with umbels of twenty or more white, bell-shaped flowers, flushed green and maroon.

Where to Grow
These tall-stemmed plants topped with large clusters of flowers add elegance to the back of the late-spring border. They are also well suited to a wild garden.

Perfect Partners
The pale flower clusters of *Nectaroscordum* look especially lovely against a dark backdrop, such as evergreens or a dark-colored fence. Short 'Magic Fountain Hybrids' delphiniums (*Delphinium* x *elatum*), peach-leaved bellflower (*Campanula persicifolia*), and low-growing hardy shrub roses such as 'J. P. Connell', 'Henry Hudson', 'John Franklin', and 'Morden Blush', planted just in front of nectaroscordum, are all winning combinations.

Puschkinia

(push-*kih*-nee-ah)
striped squill, Lebanon squill

PLANT AT A GLANCE (photos pp. 24, 116)

Type: true bulb
Flowering Time: early to mid-spring
Height: 15 to 20 cm (6 to 8 in.)
Soil: average to fertile, moist, well drained
Light: full to part sun
When to Plant: fall
How to Plant: 8 cm (3 in.) deep, 15 cm (6 in.) apart
Propagation: division, offsets, seed (also self-seeds)
Poisonous: no
Deer/Rodent Resistant: no
Good for Forcing: yes

Striped squill is a tough little bulb that comes out of hiding very early in the spring, at about the same time as its cousins Siberian squill (*Scilla sibirica*) and glory-of-the snow (*Chionodoxa* spp.). Unfazed by lingering snow and frost, striped squill thrives in regions with cold winters and cool summers, which makes it a perfect candidate for most prairie gardens. This is not surprising, since striped squill grows wild in the mountainous regions of the Middle East, frequently at elevations above 3,050 m (10,000 ft.).

The genus *Puschkinia*, which comprises the single species *Puschkinia scilloides*, was named after Count Apollos Apollosevich Mussin-Puschkin, a botanist who collected plants in the Caucasus—not, as some people believe, after Aleksandr Sergeevich Pushkin, the Russian poet much favored by Catherine the Great. A jubilant display of delicate *Puschkinia* in early spring is at least as grand as the title of its namesake, if not more so!

Portrait

Striped squill produces a pair of strap-shaped, medium green leaves that ripen quickly after blooming is complete. This is a bonus for gardeners who are discovering the ins and outs of dying bulb foliage.

As many as six squill-like flowers are borne on a short flower stalk that reaches just beyond the 15-cm (6-in.) leaves. The star-shaped blossoms are very pale blue—the color of skim milk—and individual petals are etched down the middle with a noticeable greenish blue stripe. At the center of each flower is a small but prominent little dome, formed by the filaments of the stamens. *Puschkinia scilloides* var. *libanotica* has smaller flowers and more sharply lobed petals, which are plain white, rarely striped in blue.

As with so many plants, the nomenclature for this one is a bit confusing. You will often find striped squill sold as *Puschkinia libanotica*. A ghostly white 'Alba' cultivar, minus the greenish blue stripes, is also available, but it may very well be the plain white *P. s.* var. *libanotica*. Regardless of its correct botanical name, striped squill is a "must have" for the prairie spring garden.

Where to Grow

Striped squill is an excellent candidate for naturalizing in a lawn or tucking into a rock garden. It is also attractive planted in drifts just under the edge of deciduous shrubs or along the edge of a pathway where it can be readily enjoyed. Force a handful of striped squill bulbs in a pot, and you can have an attractive centerpiece for the kitchen table while the blizzards are still raging outdoors.

Perfect Partners

Adjacent or mingling small clumps or drifts of minor bulbs such as Siberian squill (*Scilla sibirica*), snowdrops (*Galanthus* spp.), glory-of-the-snow (*Chionodoxa* spp.), and striped squill, interspersed with early-blooming primulas and hepaticas, will put on an amazing show of early spring color when not much else is blooming in the garden. What's more, the show gets better each year as the bulbs mature and multiply.

Sanguinaria
(sang-gwin-*air*-ee-ah)
bloodroot, red puccoon

PLANT AT A GLANCE (photo p. 116)

Type: rhizome
Flowering Time: spring
Height: 25 cm (10 in.)
Soil: fertile, moist, well drained
Light: full to part sun in active growth; light shade after blooming
When to Plant: fall (bare-root rhizomes); spring through fall (container-grown plants)
How to Plant: place rhizomes in ground horizontally, with growth points just below the soil's surface, 20 cm (8 in.) apart; will go dormant late in the summer without adequate moisture
Propagation: rhizome divisions, seed; divide rhizomes during dormancy, otherwise they will suffer excessive "bleeding," resulting in loss of plant vigor
Poisonous: no

Puschkinia scilloides (striped squill) (see p. 114). *Lesley Reynolds*

Sanguinaria canadensis (bloodroot). *Llyn Strelau*

Deer/Rodent Resistant: yes
Good for Forcing: no

One of the loveliest and most unusual foliage plants for the woodland garden or lightly shaded border is bloodroot (*Sanguinaria canadensis*), so-called because of the orange-red, bloodlike sap found in the plant, especially in its stems and rhizomes. Damaged rhizomes can "bleed" this sap in copious amounts. The plant derives both its botanical and common names from the sap's resemblance to blood—*sanguis* is the Latin word for blood.

Not surprisingly, bloodroot sap has been used variously in the past as a red dye for war paint and for decorative baskets and clothing. It also contains an anti-plaque, anti-gingivitis substance called sanguinarine, which is used in some modern mouth care products to control bad breath and sore gums.

Once established, bloodroot forms a delightful groundcover of distinctive gray-green foliage with deeply lobed margins. The exquisite but short-lived white flowers are a bonus in early spring.

Portrait

Bloodroot buds emerge in early spring, forming thick shoots tightly wrapped in foliage; the underside of emergent bloodroot foliage is a striking deep wine color. As the leaves unfurl, flower stems quickly shoot up to a height of 25 cm (10 in.) and produce charming solitary, white, cup-shaped flowers with eight to ten petals each and prominent golden stamens, followed by an interesting seed pod. 'Flore Pleno' (syn. 'Multiplex', 'Plena') is a choice double cultivar whose white blossoms look like miniature water lilies and last longer than its single equivalent.

As the short-lived flowers fade, bloodroot foliage continues to unfurl, mature, and transform at maturity into bold saucerlike, deeply lobed, gray-green leaves, 15 to 30 cm (6 to 12 in.) across. Left to their own devices, bloodroot rhizomes will expand to form a dense, ground-covering mat of these fascinating and highly individual leaves.

With adequate moisture, bloodroot leaves last for most of the summer before going dormant. However, if they are allowed to dry out, they will enter dormancy prematurely and, with insufficient time to replenish food supplies in the rhizome, will return with less vigor the following year.

Where to Grow
Bloodroot makes an attractive groundcover in a woodland garden or a lightly shaded rock garden.

Perfect Partners
Elegant white bloodroot flowers go well with the brilliant blue blooms of squill (*Scilla* spp.) and grape hyacinth (*Muscari* spp.). The deeply scalloped, gray-green foliage, which lingers long after the blossoms have faded, contrasts beautifully with other woodland foliage plants, such as ferns, foamflower (*Tiarella* spp.), small goatsbeard (*Aruncus aethusifolius*), ginger (*Asarum europaeum*), bunchberry (*Cornus canadensis*), and astilbe. Merrybells (*Uvularia* spp.), fairy bells (*Disporum* spp.), and twinleaf (*Jeffersonia diphylla*) also make natural partners.

Scilla
(*skee*-lah)
squill

PLANT AT A GLANCE (photos pp. 21, 24, 120)

Type: true bulb
Flowering Time: early to mid-spring
Height: 15 cm (6 in.)
Soil: average to fertile, well drained
Light: full sun to light shade
When to Plant: fall
How to Plant: 8 to 10 cm (3 to 4 in.) deep, 8 cm (3 in.) apart
Propagation: division, offsets, seed (also self-seeds)
Poisonous: yes, all parts harmful when ingested, may cause skin irritation
Deer/Rodent Resistant: yes
Good for Forcing: yes

At a time when few other plants have emerged from hibernation, the enchanting, intensely blue bells of squill lift the spirits of all prairie dwellers longing for spring. As a bonus, these hardy little treasures can be left undisturbed for years, continuing to spread and bloom happily without any work on the part of the gardener.

The genus name *Scilla* is derived from the Greek *skilla* (sea squill). At least five members of this genus, which belongs to the *Liliaceae* family, are known to have been in cultivation at the end of the sixteenth century, when the plants were used for medicinal purposes and to produce starch to stiffen Elizabethan collars.

Among the eighty or more members of the genus, *Scilla sibirica* is the most widely cultivated. Native to southern Russia, the Caucasus, and western Asia, it is among the hardiest and most desirable of spring bulbs, blooming reliably and spreading its patches of intense blue wider each year.

Portrait

Squill are prized for their racemes of dainty, bell- to star-shaped flowers. The emerald to medium green basal leaves are lance- or strap-shaped, and die back soon after flowering. Since squill will self-seed abundantly, be careful not to accidentally weed out the grasslike seedlings. Although not all members of the genus are hardy on the prairies, several have proven to be so and make valuable additions to the spring garden.

- *Scilla bifolia* (20 cm, 8 in.) bears up to ten starry, upward-facing, turquoise to violet blue flowers on each one-sided raceme. As the species name suggests, each plant produces only two leaves. Cultivars include 'Alba' (white) and 'Rosea' (pink).
- *Scilla mischtschenkoana* (syn. *S. tubergeniana*) (15 cm, 6 in.), milk squill, is the earliest-blooming hardy squill. It produces small spikes of two to six pale blue flowers, each striped with darker blue, that open up nearly flat. The flowers generally burst forth before the glossy leaves emerge.
- *Scilla sibirica* (15 cm, 6 in.), Siberian squill, bears spikes of up to six loosely arrayed, bright blue, nodding bells marked with a darker stripe on each petal. The individual flowers have six flared petals and resemble tiny fairies' caps. 'Spring Beauty' (also sold as 'Atrocaerulea') is a superb cultivar with deep violet blue flowers that are larger than those of the species. *Scilla sibirica* var. *taurica* is a lighter blue form, while *S. s.* var. *alba* is white.

Where to Grow

Plant squill in rock gardens, on banks, and beside pathways. They are perfect, easy-to-grow little plants for naturalizing under deciduous trees and shrubs in woodland gardens. Since the foliage matures quite quickly, they are a good choice for planting in turf. Drifts of squill are also charming at the front of a perennial or shrub border. Although squill benefits from spring sunshine, avoid planting it in areas that will be baked dry in summer.

Perfect Partners

Blue-flowered squill is complemented beautifully by dwarf narcissus, snowdrops (*Galanthus* spp.), glory-of-the-snow (*Chionodoxa luciliae*), and early tulips such as *Tulipa kaufmanniana* and its hybrids. In a rock garden, plant squill with brightly colored Iceland poppies (*Papaver croceum*), and rock cress (*Arabis* spp.). Gardeners who love the cool purity of a white spring garden should try *Scilla sibirica* var. *alba* in combination with white crocus, snowdrops (*Galanthus* spp.), narcissus, hepatica, and arabis.

Trillium

(*trill*-ee-um)
trillium, wakerobin

PLANT AT A GLANCE (photo p. 120)

Type: rhizome
Flowering Time: mid-spring
Height: 45 cm (18 in.)
Soil: fertile, moist, well drained
Light: light shade to part sun
When to Plant: fall (bare-root rhizomes); spring to late summer (container-grown plants); do not allow rhizomes to dry out
How to Plant: 8 cm (3 in.) deep, 30 cm (12 in.) apart
Propagation: division after foliage dies in summer, seed
Poisonous: no
Deer/Rodent Resistant: no
Good for Forcing: no

Picture a cool, green woodland glade, dappled spring sunshine filtering to the forest floor. This is the habitat of the elegant trillium. If this image clashes with your idea of a stereotypical sun-soaked prairie garden, think again. Gardeners are discovering that shade gardens not only offer escape from the searing summer heat, but also present a whole new palette of fascinating flora and foliage.

Scilla sibirica 'Spring Beauty' (Siberian squill) (see p. 117).
Liesbeth Leatherbarrow

It is possible that the genus *Trillium* was named from the Swedish word for triplet, *trilling*, by the Swedish botanist Linnaeus. Alternatively, the word may derive from the Latin words *tri* (three) and *lilium* (lily). Either way, the generic name clearly refers to the tripartite nature of the flowers and leaves. Although a few trilliums are of Asian origin, most of the over thirty species in the genus are North American natives, found in forests from coast to coast.

An old wives' tale suggests that if you pick the flower of a trillium, the plant will die. Even though this has been proven false, most gardeners likely prefer their trilliums blooming in the garden rather than in a vase.

Unfortunately, trilliums take up to six years to bloom when grown from seed, and have proven difficult to propagate by tissue culture due to fungal problems. As a result of the growing demand for these elegant woodland beauties, many plants are gathered out of the wild. It is important to the survival of these native plants that you ensure that any trilliums you purchase have been grown from cultivated stock.

Portrait

The hardiest trillium for prairie gardens is, by a happy coincidence, also among the loveliest of the genus. Like all trilliums, *Trillium grandiflorum* has three leaf-like outer sepals and three showy inner petals. The solitary, snowy white flowers have golden stamens and open to a diameter of up to 8 cm (3 in.), often fading to pale pink as they mature. The medium green, oval to circular leaves are whorled

Trillium grandiflorum (trillium). Llyn Strelau

in threes around the sturdy flower stem and often die back after blooming. *T. grandiflorum* var. *roseum* is a pink form, while 'Flore Pleno' is a striking double, white-flowered cultivar.

Avid woodland gardeners may wish to check with native plant specialists for *Trillium cernuum*, a dainty species native to northeastern Saskatchewan and Manitoba. This rare trillium bears nodding, white or pale pink flowers.

Since trilliums prefer a more acidic and humus-rich soil than is usually found in prairie gardens, incorporate plenty of compost and peat moss into the soil before planting. Left undisturbed, trilliums will slowly increase to form sizable clumps, provided they receive enough moisture. Allow fallen leaves to remain in place to protect them during the winter, particularly in areas where snow cover may be lacking.

Where to Grow
There is really only one ideal location for trilliums—the woodland garden. However, if you have a new garden with little shade from trees, try planting trilliums on the north side of a building, making sure they are watered regularly. Avoid hot, dry locations.

Perfect Partners
Surround trilliums with a carpet of blue grape hyacinths (*Muscari* spp.) or delicate shooting stars (*Dodecatheon meadia*). They also pair beautifully with the pendant blooms of fernleaf or fringed bleeding hearts (*Dicentra formosa*, *D. eximia*) and Canadian columbines (*Aquilegia canadensis*). Hostas and ferns will fill in the spaces vacated by dormant trilliums later in the summer.

Tulipa
(*tew*-lip-ah)
tulip

PLANT AT A GLANCE (photos pp. 1, 13, 16, 17, 57, 125, 126, 128, 129)

Type: true bulb
Flowering Time: early spring to early summer, depending on the type; see individual descriptions
Height: 15 to 76 cm (6 to 30 in.)
Soil: fertile, moist, well drained, dry after flowering
Light: full sun
When to Plant: fall

How to Plant: 10 cm (4 in.) deep (species), 15 cm (6 in.) deep (hybrids), 10 to 20 cm (4 to 8 in.) apart; if you are very late getting bulbs into the ground in the fall, peeling the tunic before planting allows bulbs to push roots three days sooner—tulip bulbs need a total of seven days of unfrozen soil to push roots
Propagation: division, offsets, seed
Poisonous: no
Deer/Rodent Resistant: no
Good for Forcing: yes

Today, for a very modest investment, any garden can bloom from April until June with the sumptuous shades and elegant shapes of tulips. Although large, showy cultivars remain popular, an increasing number of hardy and beautiful little species (native) tulips are popping up every spring across the prairies.

Native to the mountainous terrain of Turkey, the Caucasus, and Russian lands neighboring the Black Sea (part of the Turkish Empire of Persia in the 1500s), tulips derive their genus name from the Turkish word *tulband* (turban), describing the flower's resemblance to their national headgear. Tulips enjoy a rich cultural history in Persia, where they have been cultivated since 1000 AD.

Tulips were introduced to Europe from Turkey in 1554, and to the Netherlands in 1593, by Carolus Clusius, a renowned botanist who settled in Holland to escape religious intolerance elsewhere in Europe. It is believed that bulbs stolen from Clusius's collection laid the foundation for the tulip-growing industry in Holland.

By the seventeenth century, tulips were so popular among the rich that bulbs were considered a status symbol and traded for vast sums of money. Especially valuable were the so-called "broken" or Rembrandt tulips. They possessed unique flamed and striped markings that we now know were the result of a virus spread by aphids, but then were worth a fortune. The bulb-buying mania that flourished in Holland from 1634 to 1637 came to a rude halt in 1637 when the futures market in bulbs crashed; sadly (or deservedly?), many fortunes made speculating in tulips evaporated overnight. Surely, "Tulipomania" ranks as one of the most dubious investment schemes of all time.

Despite the hardship that followed the crash of 1637, the Dutch capitalized on their newly acquired knowledge of growing tulips, cultivating and hybridizing them so widely that there are now thousands of cultivars available.

Portrait

Tulips can be divided into two basic kinds: species (or native) and hybridized. Given acceptable growing conditions, many species tulips survive prairie winters in good shape and develop and spread into established colonies, becoming lovelier every year.

Usually, the large hybrids that are so popular among gardeners bloom their best the first year after they are planted. However, gardeners can produce good tulip blossoms year after year by following these tips.

- Fertilize heavily during growth and bloom season.
- Deadhead flowers as soon as they begin to fade so no energy is wasted making seeds.
- Leave the stalk and leaves intact until they fade and wither, so photosynthesis and food production continue to strengthen and "fatten" the bulb.
- Dig up all the bulbs in the fall and only replant the biggest, for good performance the following spring; small bulbs can be planted in a nursery bed to acquire a good size before being replanted in the flowerbed.

When choosing your bulbs, keep in mind that some hybrids of Greigii ('Red Riding Hood', 'Toronto'), Fosteriana ('Purissima', 'Red Emperor'), Praestans ('Fusilier'), Darwin ('Beauty of Apeldoorn'), Lily-flowered ('Ballade', 'Maytime', 'White Triumphator'), and Triumph ('Don Quichotte', 'Kees Nelis') tulips are much longer-lived than the rest of them; they are as close to long-lived perennial tulips as you can get.

Tulips are classified into fifteen divisions based upon origin and bloom shape. For flower variety and continuous color throughout the spring, choose a selection from early, mid, and late spring-blooming varieties. Be prepared to protect early bloomers from hard frost.

Early Spring

I.   Single Early tulips (15 to 45 cm, 6 to 18 in.) have large red, yellow, or white flowers, often margined, flamed, or flecked in a contrasting color. Interesting cultivars include 'Apricot Beauty' (salmon pink with orange margins), 'Bestseller' (copper orange), 'Christmas Dream' (cherry red, fragrant), 'Christmas Marvel' (cherry pink), 'Generaal de Wet' (golden orange, fragrant), 'Keizerskroon' (red with yellow margins), and 'Yokohama' (yellow).

II. Double Early tulips (30 to 40 cm, 12 to 16 in.) produce fully double, bowl-shaped flowers that are usually fragrant. Try 'Abba' (red, fragrant), 'Electra' (magenta), 'Monte Carlo' (golden yellow, fragrant), 'Mr. Van de Hoef' (yellow, fragrant), 'Peach Blossom' (light pink, long-lived), 'Red Carpet' (red), and 'Schoonoord' (white, fragrant).

III.   Triumph tulips (35 to 60 cm, 14 to 24 in.) are tall with large, cup-shaped flowers. Try 'Barcelona' (bright pink), 'Bellona' (golden yellow), 'Blenda' (carmine red), 'Celebration' (red), 'Couleur Cardinal' (reddish purple, fragrant), 'Don Quichotte' (purplish pink, long-lived), 'Frankfurt' (cardinal red), 'Kees Nelis' (red and yellow, long-lived), 'Lustige Witwe', also called 'Merry Widow' (red edged with white), 'Dreaming Maid' (violet edged with white), 'Gavota' (purple edged in yellow), 'Gerrit de Jongh' (red edged in white), 'Golden Melody' (yellow, long-lived), 'Negrita' (plum purple), 'Prinses Irene' (orange and purple, fragrant, long-lived), 'Salmon Pearl' (crimson rose edged with coral, fragrant), 'Valentino' (pink edged with white), and 'White Dream' (white).

IV.   Darwin Hybrid tulips (50 to 70 cm, 20 to 28 in.) have large, brightly colored flowers on tall, strong stems. Try 'Ad Rem' (scarlet edged with yellow, fragrant), 'Apeldoorn' (red, long-lived), 'Apeldoorn's Elite' (yellow and red), 'Beauty of Apeldoorn' (yellow, orange, and red striped, long-lived), 'Bienvenue' (canary yellow, flamed dark pink with greenish bases), 'Blushing Beauty' (flamed red with yellow edges), 'Daydream' (apricot orange, fragrant), 'Golden Parade' (yellow), 'Elizabeth Arden' (salmon pink), and 'Renown' (red).

Late Spring

V.   Single Late tulips (45 to 76 cm, 18 to 30 in.) comprise a variable group with a large color range. The blossoms are cup- or goblet-shaped and sometimes are produced several to a stem. Try 'Gander' (magenta red), 'Kingsblood' (cherry red), 'Union Jack' (red and white streaked), 'Queen of Night' (maroon black), and 'Blue Aimable' (lilac).

VI.   Lily-flowered tulips (45 to 65 cm, 18 to 26 in.), once called Ottoman tulips, have elegantly shaped, long-petaled, lilylike blooms, with petals gently reflexed at the tips. Try 'Akita' (red with white edges), 'Ballade' (reddish magenta with white margins, long-lived), 'Ballerina' (marigold orange, fragrant), 'Mariette' (rose pink), 'Marilyn' (white with purple flames on the outside, white with red flames on the inside), 'Maytime' (reddish violet with white edges, long-lived), 'West Point' (yellow), 'Temple of Beauty' (orange red), and 'White Triumphator' (white, long-lived).

Double Early *Tulipa* 'Monte Carlo'.
Lesley Reynolds

VII. Fringed tulips (35 to 65 cm, 14 to 26 in.), or Crispa tulips, have petals with fringed margins, usually in a different color. Interesting cultivars include 'Blue Heron' (violet purple fringed in purple, striped in white on the inside), 'Burgundy Lace' (wine red), 'Burns' (light pink, insides pinkish red with white bases and purple margins), 'Fancy Frills' (deep rose red with pale white fringes), 'Fancy Hamilton' (yellow), and 'Maja' (pale yellow).

A mix of Triumph tulips – *Tulipa* 'Negrita', 'Frankfurt', 'Valentino', and 'White Dream'.
Liesbeth Leatherbarrow

VIII. Viridiflora tulips (40 to 55 cm, 16 to 22 in.) are exceptionally long flowering and all have the color green in common. They can be solid green, edged with another color, or flamed or striped in green. Try 'Golden Artist' (golden orange with green stripes), 'Groenland' (green with pink margins), and 'Spring Green' (ivory, feathered green). These tulips are of borderline hardiness in prairie gardens.

Lily-flowered *Tulipa* 'Ballade' (front) and Double Late *T.* 'Lilac Perfection' (back).
Liesbeth Leatherbarrow

IX. Rembrandt tulips (45 to 65 cm, 18 to 26 in.), the so-called "broken" tulips, are mostly of historical interest. These cup-shaped tulips, uniquely streaked in brown, black, bronze, pink, purple, or red, were the source of fortunes won and lost during the Dutch "Tulipomania" of the 1600s. Because the streaking is

Unique and dramatically marked tulips like this one, a result of a virus spread by aphids, were highly prized during the seventeenth-century Dutch "Tulipomania." *Liesbeth Leatherbarrow*

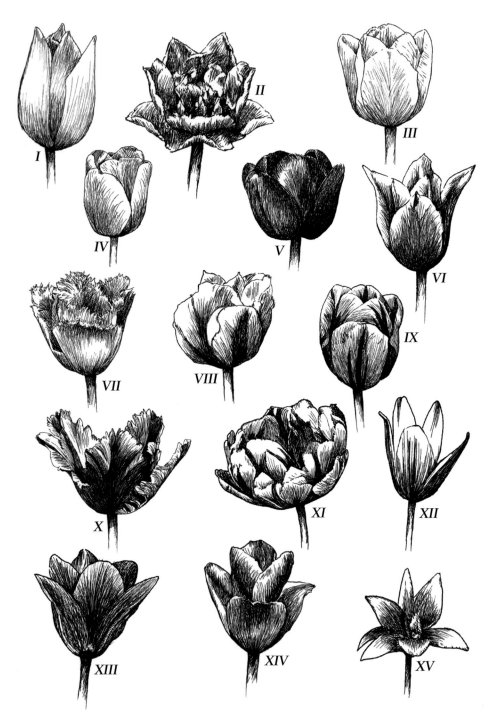

TULIP CLASSIFICATIONS I. Single Early: 'Yokohama' II. Double Early: 'Electra' III. Triumph: 'White Dream' IV. Darwin Hybrid: 'Beauty of Apeldoorn' V. Single Late: 'Queen of Night' VI. Lily-flowered: 'Ballade' VII. Fringed: 'Maja' VIII. Viridiflora: 'Spring Green' IX. Rembrandt X. Parrot XI. Double Late: 'Carnaval de Nice' XII. *Tulipa kaufmanniana* XIII. *Tulipa fosteriana* XIV. *Tulipa greigii* XV. Other Species: *Tulipa tarda*

the result of a virus, the original Rembrandts are no longer commercially available. However, because of their appeal, breeders have developed healthy tulips with similar streaking and these "Rembrandts" are often available at garden centers or through mail-order catalogues.

X. Parrot tulips (35 to 60 cm, 14 to 24 in.) have single, deeply fringed, cup-shaped blossoms in shades of white to purple, often edged or flamed in a contrasting color; these are sports (mutations) of solid-colored varieties of regular form. Plant in an area protected from the wind since their stems are not sturdy. Try 'Amethyst' (purple, rose red, and white blend), 'Apricot Parrot' (apricot pink with green stripe, fragrant), 'Estella Rijnveld' (red flamed with white, long-lived), 'Flaming Parrot' (yellow with red on a green base), and 'White Parrot' (white with green shading).

XI. Double Late tulips (35 to 60 cm, 14 to 24 in.), or peony-flowered tulips, are medium-tall tulips with large, bowl-shaped, double blooms. Try 'Allegretto' (red with yellow edge, fragrant), 'Angelique' (pale pink with rose streaks, fragrant, long-lived), 'Blue Diamond' (purple), 'Mount Tacoma' (white), 'Lilac Perfection' (lilac purple), 'Uncle Tom' (red), and 'Carnaval de Nice' (white streaked with dark red).

Species and their Hybrids

XII. *Tulipa kaufmanniana* (25 cm, 10 in.) are aptly named waterlily tulips for the open-bowl shape of their lovely creamy yellow and red blooms that appear in early spring. This robust species has gray-green, slightly wavy leaves. Its hybrids frequently have purple-brown striped or mottled leaves. Outstanding named varieties include 'Fashion' (orange), 'Stressa' (yellow), 'Showwinner' (red), 'Shakespeare' (red with yellow base), 'Scarlet Baby' (scarlet red), and 'Heart's Delight' (red and yellow, long-lived).

XIII. *Tulipa fosteriana* (50 cm, 20 in.) comprise a long-stemmed group of early spring-blooming tulips with the largest flowers of any tulips, species or hybrid; the big red blossoms of the species are 20 cm (8 in.) across. Some hybrids to try are 'Purissima', also called 'White Emperor' (white, fragrant, long-lived), 'Juan' (orange-red with golden yellow base), 'Yellow Empress' (yellow), and 'Red Emperor', also called 'Madame Lefeber' (glossy red, long-lived).

XIV. *Tulipa greigii* (30 cm, 12 in.) produces orange-scarlet flowers in early to mid-spring; many feature purple-striped foliage. Look for 'Red Riding Hood' (scarlet, long-lived), 'Pinocchio' (yellow striped with red), 'Sweet Lady' (deep salmon pink), and 'Toronto' (salmon pink, long-lived).

Tulipa greigii 'Sweet Lady'. *Lesley Reynolds*

XV. Other species and their varieties or hybrids
- *Tulipa acuminata* (45 cm, 18 in.) is an unusual light red or yellow tulip with slender, spiky petals and linear, gray-green leaves.
- *Tulipa batalinii* (30 cm, 12 in.) produces bowl-shaped, pale yellow flowers and has linear, gray-green leaves with red margins. 'Bright Gem' is a lovely cultivar.

Tulipa batalinii 'Bright Gem'. *Llyn Strelau*

- *Tulipa clusiana* (23 cm, 9 in.), produces blossoms that are rosy red on the outside and creamy white inside.
- *Tulipa eichleri* (30 cm, 12 in.) has scarlet flowers with jet black centers, outlined in yellow in early spring.
- *Tulipa kolpakowskiana* (15 cm, 6 in.) has narrow leaves with wavy margins and yellow, cup-shaped, fragrant flowers marked crimson, orange, or olive green on the outside, in mid-spring.
- *Tulipa linifolia* (15 cm, 6 in.) has linear gray-green leaves edged with red, and bowl-shaped red flowers with black bases.
- *Tulipa praestans* (30 cm, 12 in.) produces clusters of scarlet red flowers in mid-spring, and has pale green leaves edged in dark red. Try 'Fusilier' (scarlet red, multi-flowered, long-lived), 'Van Tubergen's Variety' (orange scarlet), and 'Unicum' (scarlet red with cream and green variegated foliage).
- *Tulipa pulchella* (15 cm, 6 in.) produces large, cup-shaped blossoms that form a flat star when fully open; the early spring blossoms come in shades of magenta

pink, violet, or white. Look for the delightful cultivar 'Persian Pearl' (rose red with yellow centers).

- *Tulipa tarda* (syn. *T. dasystemon*) produces shiny, lance-shaped, bright green leaves and clusters of star-shaped, fragrant, golden yellow flowers with petals tipped in white in early spring.
- *Tulipa turkestanica* (30 cm, 12 in.) produces clusters of star-shaped blossoms in early spring that are gray-green on the outside and white with yellow petal bases on the inside.

Tulip Bloom Sequence

Early Spring
- *Tulipa eichleri, T. fosteriana, T. greigii, T. kaufmanniana, T. praestans, T. pulchella, T. tarda, T. turkestanica,* Single Early, Double Early

Mid-spring
- *Tulipa kolpakowskiana, T. linifolia,* Triumph, Darwin Hybrid

Late Spring
- *Tulipa acuminata, T. clusiana,* Single Late, Lily-flowered, Parrot, Double Late, Rembrandt type, Fringed, Viridiflora

Where to Grow

The short species tulips and their cultivars are perfect fare for well-drained, sunny rock gardens. They also are suitable for planting at the front of mixed or perennial borders or for naturalizing beneath deciduous shrubs and trees. Tall hybrid tulips lend an elegant and formal touch to flower borders. They can be planted en masse in drifts at an angle to the flowerbed's edge or in precise bands of constant width at the front. Mass planting is most effective in blocks of a single color or two or three complementary colors.

Perfect Partners

Group species tulips with similar bloom times in rock gardens, with blue-flowered Siberian squill (*Scilla sibirica*), striped squill (*Puschkinia scilloides*), glory-of-the-snow (*Chionodoxa luciliae*), and various dwarf narcissus as

Tulipa tarda (dasystemon tulip). Llyn Strelau

companions. Hybrid tulips are impressive when planted in front of evergreen trees and shrubs or spring-flowering shrubs such as double flowering plum (*Prunus triloba* 'Multiplex'), purpleleaf sand cherry (*Prunus* x *cistena*), and spirea. They can also be bunched with perennials that bloom at the same time, such as columbine (*Aquilegia* spp.), bleeding heart (*Dicentra* spp.), spurge (*Euphorbia polychroma*), and iris. Lady's mantle (*Alchemilla* spp.) and daylily (*Hemerocallis* spp.) are also good companions.

Borderline Bulbs

When we talked to prairie gardeners about which bulbs were succeeding in their gardens, we were surprised to find that some of them, according to conventional zone ratings, really had no business growing in our tough climate. Of course, the bulbs described here won't grow in every prairie garden; a lot depends on particular microclimates. However, they all benefit from a good layer of mulch to help them through the winter and many require protection from late-spring hard frosts. All are growing happily somewhere on the prairies, so if you would like to expand your bulb repertoire to include more than the tried and true, give these a try.

Anemone
(a-*nem*-oh-nee)
windflower

PLANT AT A GLANCE (photo p. 132)

Type: tuber or rhizome
Flowering Time: late spring for two to four weeks, except *Anemone coronaria*, which must be grown as a tender summer-flowering bulb
Height: 5 to 30 cm (2 to 12 in.)
Soil: average to fertile (*Anemone blanda, A. coronaria*); fertile, moist (*A. canadensis*); fertile, moist, well drained (*A. nemerosa*)
Light: full to part sun (*Anemone blanda, A. coronaria*); part sun to light shade (*A. canadensis, A. nemerosa*)
When to Plant: fall (hardy tubers and rhizomes), spring (tender tubers)
How to Plant: 8 cm (3 in.) deep, 10 cm (4 in.) apart; soak tubers in lukewarm water for twenty-four hours as soon as you receive them and then plant them immediately, otherwise blooms may be sparse or non-existent; plant tubers indented side up or on their sides if you can't tell the top from the bottom
Propagation: division, offsets, seed (also self-seeds)
Poisonous: yes, sap may cause skin irritation
Deer/Rodent Resistant: no
Good for Forcing: yes, *Anemone blanda* only

Delightful daisylike anemones, or windflowers, are cheerful spring-flowering plants perfectly suited to an informal prairie garden. The saucer-shaped flowers with bright golden stamens are available in a variety of colors that glow at the front of a sunny border or brighten a woodland landscape.

The genus *Anemone* is said to have derived its name from Naaman, the Semitic version of Adonis, the Greek vegetation god who represented the annual growth cycle. Like many other flowers that have their genesis in the spilled blood of mythic heroes, anemones are said to have sprung from the blood of the mortally wounded Naaman (Adonis). There is also a legend that red anemones arose from the blood of Christ dripping from the cross.

Although some of the approximately 120 anemone species have fibrous rootstocks, many are tuberous or rhizomatous. Not all are hardy in cold climates, but three species are good choices for prairie gardeners. *Anemone blanda*, Grecian windflower, is native to southeastern Europe and Asia Minor, while *A. nemerosa*, wood anemone, is found in European woodlands and pastures. *A. canadensis*, meadow anemone, is a North American native partial to moist meadows, creeksides, and low-lying areas.

Of the three species, *Anemone blanda* will tolerate the most sun and summer drought. It is endangered in the wild, so make sure that the tubers you buy are labeled "Bulbs grown from cultivated stock."

Adventurous gardeners may wish to try the flamboyant poppy anemone, *Anemone coronaria*, a tender tuber that must be grown as a summer-flowering bulb on the prairies. These tubers should be planted indoors in pots and moved outside to a sunny, sheltered area after all risk of frost has passed. This anemone is widely used by florists in cut flower arrangements, but be forewarned: home gardeners may not be able to duplicate the spectacular blooms achieved in the controlled conditions of florists' greenhouses.

Portrait

Anemones are characterized by medium to dark green, palmate, deeply divided leaves that tend to die back after flowering.

- *Anemone blanda* (15 cm, 6 in.), Grecian windflower, grows from small, knobby tubers and bears white, pink, or blue flowers up to 4 cm (1.5 in.) across, one flower per stem. The blooms close at night and during cloudy weather. There are several good cultivars, including 'Charmer' (deep rose), 'Blue Star' (pale blue), 'Ingramii' (deep blue), 'Pink Star' (bright pink), 'Radar' (magenta to red with white centers), 'Violet Star' (deep amethyst), and 'White Splendor' (white with pink flush on outside).
- *Anemone canadensis* (15 cm, 6 in.), meadow anemone, spreads by rhizomes. The flowers, from one to three per stem, resemble white buttercups with yellow centers and can reach 5 cm (2 in.) across.

- *Anemone coronaria* (30 cm, 12 in.), poppy anemone, grows from tender tubers. This species boasts single or double, red, blue, purple, or white flowers with dark stamens. The best-known cultivars are in the single-flowered De Caen group and the double-flowered St. Brigid group.

Anemone blanda (Grecian windflower) and miniature narcissus.
Liesbeth Leatherbarrow

- *Anemone nemerosa* (15 cm, 6 in.), wood anemone, spreads by rhizomes and has starry, white flowers tinged with pink, up to 2.5 cm (1 in.) across. Look for these lovely cultivars: 'Allenii' (lavender blue), 'Atrocaerulea' (deep blue-purple), 'Bracteata Pleniflora' (semi-double, white flowers with green-tipped tepals [petals and sepals]), 'Flore Plena' (double white), 'Robinsoniana' (pale lavender with gray exterior), 'Rosea' (red-purple), 'Vestal' (white with a central boss of many tepals).
- *Anemone ranunculoides* (5 to 10 cm, 2 to 4 in.), a rhizomatous anemone perfect for naturalizing, bears solitary yellow blossoms.

Where to Grow
Low-growing anemones are ideal for the front of perennial borders, as an edging along pathways, and for underplanting deciduous shrubs. *Anemone nemerosa* and *A. canadensis* are particularly suited for naturalizing in a woodland garden, while *A. blanda* is a good candidate for the rock garden.

Perfect Partners
Plant anemones in front of late-blooming tulips or dwarf irises (*Iris* x *pumila*). In partly shaded gardens enjoy them with ajuga, forget-me-nots (*Myosotis* spp.), primulas, and sweet woodruff (*Galium odoratum*), or simply place them against a background of lacy green ferns. Since the foliage of anemones generally goes dormant during the summer, plant them beside later-blooming perennials that will fill in the gaps. Cranesbill (*Geranium* spp.), coral bells (*Heuchera* spp.), astilbe, foamflower (*Tiarella* spp.), and lady's mantle (*Alchemilla mollis*) are all attractive choices.

Camassia

(ca-*mass*-ee-ya)

camass, quamash

PLANT AT A GLANCE (photo p. 136)

Type: true bulb
Flowering Time: late spring to early summer
Height: 20 to 130 cm (8 to 50 in.)
Soil: average to fertile, moist, well drained
Light: full to part sun
When to Plant: fall
How to Plant: 10 to 13 cm (4 to 5 in.) deep, 15 cm (6 in.) apart
Propagation: division, offsets, seed; offsets are few in number so it is best to leave bulbs undisturbed
Poisonous: yes, bulbs harmful when ingested raw, edible when cooked
Deer/Rodent Resistant: yes
Good for Forcing: no

Camass is a North American native plant found in damp meadows or along streams in partly shaded woodlands from northern California to British Columbia, and in the Rockies inland to Utah and Montana. The large bulbs of one species of this charming wildflower, *Camassia quamash*, were harvested as a source of food by the Nez Percé and other people living in the Pacific northwest. The Native peoples boiled or roasted the bulbs, which are poisonous when raw. Lewis and Clark were served camass bulbs by the people they encountered on their westward journey into the Oregon Territory in 1804. The name "camass" is from the Nootka word *kamas*, which is a variation of *quamash*.

Prairie gardeners who have admired the hazy blue spikes of camass flowers in western mountain meadows will be pleased to know that it has been successfully grown in some prairie gardens. However, as with all plants of borderline hardiness in this area, care must be taken to ensure that its cultural requirements are met. Although camass is hardy to -30° C (-22° F), it requires ample snow cover or a deep layer of mulch to make it through a prairie winter. Plant it in a sheltered location where the soil remains moist, but not waterlogged, in sun or part sun. Camass will tolerate slightly drier conditions during summer dormancy, but is far from drought tolerant.

Portrait

Camass bears airy or dense spikes of star- or cup-shaped, blue, white, or violet flowers with yellow stamens. Opening from the bottom up in late spring, the long-lasting flowers are ideal for flower arrangements. The long, narrow, keel-shaped basal leaves die back in the summer after flowering.

Camass is not readily available in garden centers, so gardeners may need to order bulbs from specialized catalogues. Look for the following species.

- *Camassia cusickii* (90 cm, 36 in.) produces pale blue flowers on strong stems. Each flower measures up to 4 cm (1.5 in.) across, and large flower heads may contain up to one hundred individual flowers that open over a long period of time. This native of northeastern Oregon has blue-green, wavy-edged leaves. The cultivar 'Zwanenburg' has deep blue flowers.
- *Camassia leichtlinii* (60 to 130 cm, 24 to 50 in.) is the tallest camass and an excellent garden species. The 6 to 8-cm (2.5 to 3-in.) diameter flowers vary in color from white to deep purple-blue. There are several cultivars, including 'Alba' (white), 'Semiplena' (sterile, semi-double, with narrow creamy petals), and 'Electra' (lavender). *C. l.* subsp. *suksdorfii* has blue to violet flowers, while *C. l.* subsp. *suksdorfii* 'Blue Danube' produces lavender violet flowers.
- *Camassia quamash* (syn. *C. esculenta*) (20 to 60 cm, 8 to 24 in.) produces spikes of shallow, cup-shaped, blue flowers 3 to 6 cm (1.25 to 2.5 in.) across. Cultivars are 'Orion' and 'San Juan' (both dark blue).

Where to Grow
Try to find a spot in the garden that mimics the natural habitat of this wildflower. Camass is lovely naturalized in a moist meadow or planted beside a pond. It is also suitable for a border, provided the soil is kept adequately moist.

Perfect Partners
Plant camass with late-flowering tulips or group it with other moisture-loving plants, such as globeflower (*Trollius* spp.), monarda, yellow flag iris (*Iris pseudacorus*), blue flag iris (*Iris versicolor*), or even a 'Polar Bear' willow (*Salix silicola*). To disguise the dying foliage, plant camass near Siberian iris (*Iris sibirica*) or daylilies (*Hemerocallis* spp.).

Eranthis
(air-*ann*-this)
winter aconite

PLANT AT A GLANCE (photo p. 137)

Type: tuber
Flowering Time: early spring
Height: 5 to 10 cm (2 to 4 in.)
Soil: fertile, moist, well drained
Light: full to part sun
When to Plant: early fall, by mid-September at the latest; tubers dry out very easily, so soak in lukewarm water for twenty-four hours as soon as you receive them and then plant immediately, otherwise blooms may be sparse or non-existent
How to Plant: 8 cm (3 in.) deep, 8 cm (3 in.) apart
Propagation: division, seed (also self-seeds)
Poisonous: yes, all parts harmful when ingested, may cause skin irritation
Deer/Rodent Resistant: yes
Good for Forcing: yes

Winter aconites (*Eranthis hyemalis*) are small woodland treasures that quickly naturalize to form a golden carpet in the early spring garden. Growing no taller than 10 cm (4 in.), they produce yellow, buttercup-like blossoms nestled in a broad collar of shiny green leaves that hug the ground.

The genus name *Eranthis* derives from two Greek words—*er* (spring) and *anthos* (flower)—and so appropriately translates as "flower of spring." Because of its early-flowering habit, winter aconite was also often called "New Year's gifts" in years gone by. The citizens of nineteenth-century England believed that winter aconites would only grow where Roman soldiers had shed blood, which resulted in the popular common names of Roman soldiers or Romans being given to this diminutive plant.

Portrait

Winter aconites produce a single, golden yellow blossom on a 10-cm (4-in.), upright stem. The blossom stays curled shut in a tight ball on cloudy days, but when the sun comes out, it opens into a cheerful, upward-facing, cup-shaped flower, 3 cm (1.25 in.) across. It looks like, and is, a member of the buttercup family (*Ranunculaceae*). Just below the flower is a clownlike collar or ruff of contrasting, bright green, deeply incised leaves. The foliage ripens quickly and usually disappears by mid-summer, so is never really an eyesore in the garden.

Eranthis cilicica produces slightly larger, deeper yellow flowers than *E. hyemalis*, and bronzy green foliage when it first emerges from the ground.

Where to Grow

Because winter aconite is such an early bloomer, plant it in a spot in the garden that doesn't thaw too quickly in spring. Winter aconite grows well under deciduous shrubs or trees where they benefit from direct or filtered

Camassia leichtlinii (camass, quamash) (see p. 133). *Llyn Strelau*

sunlight before the shrubs and trees have leafed out, and from dappled shade later in the season. Under ideal conditions, these plants naturalize easily, spreading quickly to form large colonies by underground stems or by self-seeding.

Winter aconite is also suitable for planting in rock garden crevices, and surprisingly, makes a good container plant, although it must experience the equivalent of winter cold to produce blossoms when it is container grown.

Perfect Partners

The winter aconite looks lovely partnered with snowdrops (*Galanthus* spp.), early-flowering crocuses, *Iris reticulata*, and hellebores (*Helleborus*).

Eremurus

(er-e-*mew*-rus)
foxtail lily

PLANT AT A GLANCE (photo p. 137)

Type: tuberous root
Flowering Time: late spring to early summer
Height: 1 to 2.5 m (3.3 to 8 ft.)
Soil: average to fertile, sandy, well drained
Light: full to part sun
When to Plant: fall, as soon as possible after they have been purchased
How to Plant: 10 to 15 cm (4 to 6 in.) deep, 45 to 60 cm (18 to 24 in.) apart; handle brittle roots gently, place crown on a cone of soil, spreading roots out around it
Propagation: division, seed; divide infrequently as foxtail lilies dislike disturbance
Poisonous: no
Deer/Rodent Resistant: no
Good for Forcing: no

Few flowers can rival the impressive bloom spikes of *Eremurus*, the foxtail lily. Also called desert candle and king's spear, this magnificent tuberous-

rooted plant is native to grasslands and semi-desert regions in
western and central Asia.

Foxtail lilies do require some
coddling to make it through a
typical prairie winter, and
gardeners must take care to cover
the emerging flower stalks on
chilly spring nights to prevent
damage from late hard frosts.
However, all those who have
succeeded in overwintering these

Eranthis hyemalis (winter aconite) (see p. 134). *Adam Gibbs*

splendid plants will agree it is well worth the effort. Not only are foxtail
lilies the most spectacular vertical accent plants of the early-summer
border, but they are also beautiful and long-lasting cut flowers.

Portrait

Foxtail lilies grow from brittle tuberous roots formed of a central crown
with radiating roots. The strap- or lance-shaped leaves grow in rosettes,
from which emerge leafless flower stalks, one per crown. The upper half
of each unbranched flower stalk is densely packed with countless 1.5 to
2.5-cm (0.5 to 1-in.), star-shaped flowers that open from the bottom of
the stem upward, truly giving each spike the look of a floral fox's tail. The
foliage dies back after blooming.

There are several *Eremurus*
species and cultivars worthy of trial
in prairie gardens. *Eremurus robus-
tus* (1.8 to 2.5 m, 6 to 8 ft.), a native
of Turkestan, is the tallest foxtail
lily. It has pale pink flowers with
yellow stamens. Somewhat shorter
species include *E. stenophyllus* (syn.
E. bungei) (1 m, 3.3 ft.), with golden
yellow flowers that fade to orange;
the white-flowered *E. himalaicus*
(1.2 m, 4 ft.); and *E. aitchisonii* (syn.
E. elwesii) (1 to 1.5 m, 3.3 to 5 ft.),
a pink-flowered species.

Several hybrid series of foxtail
lilies are grouped under *Eremurus* x
isabellinus. Among the best known
are the Shelford hybrids (1.2 to 1.5 m,
4 to 5 ft.), available in shades of white,
pink, yellow, and orange and white.

Eremurus x *isabellinus* 'Rexona' (foxtail lily).
Dugald Cameron, Gardenimport

Named cultivars include 'Isobel' (rose pink touched with orange) and 'Rosalind' (bright pink). Also available in catalogues are the Ruiter hybrids (up to 2 m, 6 ft.), such as 'Cleopatra' (orange-pink), 'Fatamorgana' (white to cream), 'Image' (yellow), 'Moneymaker' (bright yellow maturing to orange), 'Pinocchio' (gold orange), and 'Rexona' (apricot pink).

Where to Grow
Foxtail lilies are eye-catching accents for the back of the early-summer border. Plant them in a sheltered spot where they will be protected from strong winds.

Perfect Partners
Evergreens are an attractive backdrop for all colors of foxtail lilies. Daylilies (*Hemerocallis* spp. and hybrids) or Siberian iris (*Iris sibirica*), also early summer bloomers, may be planted in front of foxtail lilies to complement their striking blooms and also to hide their dying foliage. Other suggestions for perennial companions include yellow loosestrife (*Lysimachia punctata*), *Penstemon digitalis* 'Husker Red', and lady's mantle (*Alchemilla mollis*).

Erythronium
(e-rith-*roan*-ee-um)
dog's-tooth violet, trout lily

PLANT AT A GLANCE (photo p. 140)

Type: corm
Flowering Time: late spring to early summer
Height: 20 to 30 cm (8 to 12 in.)
Soil: fertile, moist, well drained
Light: full to part sun in early spring, light shade after blooming
When to Plant: early fall (bare corms), plant immediately after purchase as the corms dry out very easily; spring through fall (container-grown plants)
How to Plant: 5 to 8 cm (2 to 3 in.) deep, 10 to 13 cm (4 to 5 in.) apart; keep the root run cool and moist at all times, even during dormancy
Propagation: division, seed (also self-seeds)
Poisonous: no
Deer/Rodent Resistant: yes
Good for Forcing: no

The lilylike flowers of the dog's-tooth violet, a mostly North American native plant, are every bit as lovely as true lily blossoms. However, because of their diminutive stature, gardeners must get up close and personal to fully appreciate their delicate beauty. Not often grown in prairie gardens, these plants are reputedly hardy to Zone 3 or 4, and given the conditions they prefer, established colonies should provide a welcome spot of color in the spring. The challenge lies in establishing such colonies.

This woodland plant's botanical name has its roots in the Greek word for red—*erythros*—in reference either to the red flowers of some European species or to the reddish mottling that is so prevalent in the foliage of many North American species. As for the string of common names assigned *Erythronium*, it is ironic that most focus on describing an aspect of its leaves. After all, there are only two of them. Fawn lily and trout lily refer to the distinctive leaf mottling, whereas adder's tongue and lamb's tongue refer to the leaf shape. Avalanche lily is descriptive of a species that comes into flower just as the snow starts to melt.

Portrait

Regardless of the species, nodding *Erythronium* blossoms are small replicas of larger lily blossoms. They all have six-pointed, recurved tepals (petals and sepals) that reveal a set of prominent stamens, and come in colors that range from purple, violet, and pink, through yellow and white. The flowers are borne on bare stems, sometimes singly and sometimes in clusters of four or five.

Bare stems are clad in a pair of broad, tongue-shaped, leathery leaves that may be colored a simple green or elaborately mottled in contrasting dark colors.

Erythronium dens-canis, the true dog's-tooth violet and the most commonly available species, produces solitary flowers in shades of rich pink, rose, and lilac, and foliage strongly mottled in brown and bluish green. Cultivars to look for include 'Lilac Wonder' (purple with brown spots at the base of each tepal forming a noticeable ring), 'Pink Perfection' (pink), 'Purple King' (plum with white and brown stripes in the center), 'Snowflake' (white), and 'White Splendour' (white with brown spots in the center). The vigorous *E. tuolumnense* 'Pagoda' produces from four to five golden yellow blooms per stem with a brown, central ring, and mottled foliage.

Several other *Erythronium* species may be obtained from mail-order companies (e.g., *E. americanum*, *E. grandiflorum*, *E. oregonum*, and *E. revolutum*), but have yet to be routinely tested in prairie gardens. They are all worth a try, but keep in mind that these woodland plants may take several years to become established and flower satisfactorily.

Erythronium dens-canis (dog's-tooth violet).
Llyn Strelau

Where to Grow

Plant *Erythronium* in woodland gardens beside a pathway, in lightly shaded borders or rock gardens, or under deciduous trees and shrubs. Plant in large numbers to form an eye-catching colony; this is especially important for the single-flowered species.

Perfect Partners

Many woodland foliage plants make excellent companions for *Erythronium*, complementing their distinctive leaves in spring and early summer, and stepping in to hide ripening foliage later in the season. Plants such as foamflower (*Tiarella* spp.), small goatsbeard (*Aruncus aethusifolius*), ginger (*Asarum europaeum*), bunchberry (*Cornus canadensis*), and astilbe are all good choices. Mounded clusters of mature hepatica leaves also make a nice contrast.

Hyacinthoides

(hy-ah-sin-*thoy*-dees)
bluebell

PLANT AT A GLANCE (photo p. 141)

Type: true bulb
Flowering Time: late spring
Height: 30 to 45 cm (12 to 18 in.)
Soil: fertile, moist, well drained
Light: light shade to part sun
When to Plant: fall; plant immediately after purchase as bulbs have no protective tunic and dry out quickly
How to Plant: 10 cm (4 in.) deep, 10 to 15 cm (4 to 6 in.) apart
Propagation: division, offsets, seed
Poisonous: yes, all parts harmful when ingested, may cause skin irritation
Deer/Rodent Resistant: no
Good for Forcing: no

In the familiar, romanticized version of the English countryside, the woods are positively awash with bluebells every spring. In many places in Britain this is close to the truth; in fact, the English bluebell, *Hyacinthoides non-*

scripta, is a spreading European native frowned upon by some British gardeners as being too invasive. If only it were as vigorous on the prairies! The English bluebell and its Spanish cousin, *Hyacinthoides hispanica*, are bulbs for the adventurous gardener and far from a sure bet for prairie gardens. However, given the right microclimate, prairie gardeners just might be able to pull off a little patch of "Merrie Olde England" on the prairies.

Botanists have bounced these little bulbs from genus to genus: once they were *Scilla*, then *Endymion*, and finally (one hopes) *Hyacinthoides*, which means hyacinth-like.

Portrait

The English bluebell is a native of western Europe much beloved for its fragrant, narrowly bell-shaped flowers. Each arching raceme bears from six to twelve blue, white, or pink blooms, 1.5 to 2 cm (0.5 to 0.75 in.) long. The lance-shaped leaves are glossy and dark green, turning yellow as they mature. English bluebells must be planted in soil heavily amended with organic material that is kept evenly moist. They will not tolerate hot, dry locations, so plant them where they will receive light or dappled shade.

Hyacinthoides hispanica (bluebell). *Lesley Reynolds*

More suited to hot summers than the English bluebell, the Spanish bluebell hails from Spain, Portugal, and North Africa. The bell-shaped flowers have reflexed petals and are wider than English bluebells. Up to fifteen unscented, blue, white, or pink flowers, 2 cm (0.75 in.) long, are spaced evenly around erect stems. The glossy, dark green leaves are strap-shaped and wider than those of the English bluebell. There are several Spanish bluebell cultivars, including 'Excelsior' (blue violet flowers with paler blue stripes), 'La Grandesse' (white), 'Blue Bird' (dark blue), and 'Rosabella' (violet pink). English and Spanish bluebells naturally hybridize in the wild and most cultivars are in fact hybrids of the two species. Although Spanish bluebells will tolerate drier and less fertile soil than English bluebells, they are still only of borderline hardiness on the prairies. It is advisable to plant them in part sun to light shade in soil amended with organic matter. Give them plenty of moisture in spring while they are actively growing.

Where to Grow

Bluebells are traditional favorites for naturalized and woodland gardens; in ideal conditions they will spread by seed and bulb offsets. They are also suitable for shady areas of a rock garden or in a border sheltered by perennials, shrubs, or groundcovers.

Perfect Partners

Plant bluebells with late-flowering tulips (*Tulipa*), grape hyacinth (*Muscari* spp.), primulas, pulmonaria, and leopard's bane (*Doronicum* spp.). Shade-loving perennials such as hostas, ferns, and astilbe will help disguise the yellowing foliage.

Hyacinthus
(hie-ah-*sin*-thuss)
hyacinth

PLANT AT A GLANCE (photos p. 57, 59, 144)

Type: true bulb
Flowering Time: mid-spring
Height: 25 cm (10 in.)
Soil: average to fertile, well drained
Light: full to part sun
When to Plant: fall; plant by mid-September to establish good roots before freeze-up
How to Plant: 15 cm (6 in.) deep, 15 cm (6 in.) apart
Propagation: division, offsets
Poisonous: yes, all parts harmful when ingested, may cause skin irritation
Deer/Rodent Resistant: yes
Good for Forcing: yes

According to Greek myth, Hyacinth was a beautiful youth beloved by both the god Apollo and Zephyrus, the west wind. One day, as Apollo was teaching Hyacinth to throw the discus, the jealous Zephyrus blew the discus back into the boy's head, killing him. Apollo caused the lovely flower that we now know as the hyacinth to spring from the youth's spilled blood.

The wild *Hyacinthus orientalis*, the parent species from which all cultivars ultimately descend, bears dainty, fragrant, blue flowers in loose spikes—quite unlike the fat inflorescences that characterize most modern hyacinths. Although some gardeners love these showy, strongly perfumed blooms, others would happily settle for the sweet simplicity of the original species.

Native to Turkey, Syria, Lebanon, and Iran, hyacinths were brought to Europe from Turkey in the late sixteenth century. They were grown in Padua, the site of one of Europe's first botanical gardens, and became so popular that by 1725 there were two thousand cultivars.

Hyacinths are not generally considered hardy on the prairies, but some gardeners in the region have successfully overwintered them. The bulbs are reputedly hardy to -34° C (-30° F), but the flower spikes may require protection from hard spring frosts. If you have no luck with them in the garden, they are among the easiest and most rewarding bulbs to force indoors for winter color and fragrance.

Portrait

Hybrid hyacinths produce wide, straplike, bright green leaves and a stiff flower stalk bearing dense spikes of strongly scented, waxy, star-shaped flowers. The flowers are usually single, although there are a few double cultivars, and are available in a rainbow of colors, including white, red, salmon, pink, yellow, purple, violet, and blue. Some cultivars even feature petals edged or striped with lighter or darker shades.

There are many fine cultivars to choose from, but the following are sure to please hyacinth devotees. Try 'Carnegie' (single white), 'City of Haarlem' (single yellow), 'Delft Blue' (single pale blue), 'Gipsy Queen' (single salmon apricot), 'Hollyhock' (double crimson red), 'Jan Bos' (single scarlet red), 'Lady Derby' (single rose pink), 'Ostara' (single violet blue), 'Princess Maria Christina' (single apricot), and 'Queen of the Pinks' (single deep pink).

Because they are very top heavy and susceptible to weather damage, double-flowered hyacinths generally require support. Expect hyacinth blooms to become looser and less showy after the first season of bloom, when they grow to more closely resemble their graceful wild parent. Some gardeners actually prefer this more relaxed appearance, but if you have formal plantings you may wish to replace the bulbs every year or two.

Where to Grow

Hyacinths are traditionally mass-planted in ribbons or patterned designs in formal bulb beds where the density of the blooms results in a bold block of color. However, hyacinth bulbs are expensive and since they are considered borderline on the prairies, this may be a risky venture. Prairie gardeners are better advised to plant them in groups of six to ten in a mixed border where shrubs and early emerging perennials will soften their rather stiff aspect. Make sure you locate them near a path where you can readily enjoy their sweet fragrance.

Perfect Partners

All colors of hyacinths look stunning with grape hyacinth (*Muscari* spp.), and mid-spring flowering tulips (*Tulipa*) and narcissus. Blue hyacinths are lovely paired with the dainty yellow flowers of *Primula veris* or 'Wanda' hybrid primulas (*Primula* x *juliae* 'Wanda'), or even with leopard's bane (*Doronicum* spp.) as a cheerful backdrop. Pansies (*Viola* x *wittrockiana*) and violas are also fine companions to plant at the feet of hyacinths.

Ixiolirion

(iks-ee-oh-*leer*-ee-on)
ixia lily

Hyacinthus (hyacinth) (see p. 142). *Liesbeth Leatherbarrow*

PLANT AT A GLANCE (photo p. 145)

Type: true bulb
Flowering Time: late spring
Height: 25 to 40 cm (10 to 16 in.)
Soil: average to fertile, well drained
Light: full sun
When to Plant: fall
How to Plant: 15 cm (6 in.) deep, 15 cm (6 in.) apart
Propagation: division, offsets, seed
Poisonous: no
Deer/Rodent Resistant: no
Good for Forcing: yes

Ixiolirion is another one of those "pushing the limits" bulbs that prairie gardeners delight in pulling through the winter against all odds. *Ixiolirion tataricum* (syn. *I. montanum, I. pallasii*), the Tatar or Siberian lily, is the most commonly available species. Prairie bulb enthusiasts feel that, given its Siberian homeland, this bulb should be hardy enough for the prairies, and they see growing it as an irresistible challenge.

Portrait

Ixiolirion tataricum bears sprays of funnel-shaped flowers in shades of lavender or violet blue. The six-petaled, lilylike blooms are 3 to 5 cm (1.25 to 2 in.) long, with a dark stripe on each petal. Up to ten flowers may be borne on each slender, branched stem. The medium green, basal leaves are lance shaped and disappear quickly after flowering.

In its native habitat *Ixiolirion tataricum* is adapted to spring moisture and a warm, dry summer dormancy. Like other borderline bulbs, it benefits from an 8 to 10-cm (3 to 4-in.) layer of organic mulch for winter protection.

Where to Grow

Plant *Ixiolirion tataricum* in a sheltered, sunny area where it will be protected from late-spring frosts. Grow it in clumps in rock gardens or in drifts at the front of a perennial or mixed border. The flowers are grown commercially for the cut-flower market, so are a natural for the cutting garden.

Ixiolirion tataricum (ixia lily). *Llyn Strelau*

Perfect Partners

Choose other sun-loving plants that bloom in late spring. In the rock garden, *Ixiolirion tataricum* is enhanced by the white flowers of perennial candytuft (*Iberis sempervirens*) or pink- or white-flowered rock cress (*Arabis caucasica*). Late-flowering tulips (*Tulipa*) and *Iris pumila* hybrids are colorful border companions.

Leucojum
(loo-*ko*-jum)
snowflake

PLANT AT A GLANCE (photo p. 148)

Type: true bulb
Flowering Time: early spring (*L. vernum*); late spring and early summer (*L. aestivum*)
Height: 20 to 45 cm (8 to 18 in.)
Soil: fertile, moist, well drained
Light: full to part sun
When to Plant: fall
How to Plant: 5 to 8 cm (2 to 3 in.) deep, 10 to 15 cm (4 to 6 in.) apart
Propagation: division, offsets
Poisonous: no
Deer/Rodent Resistant: no
Good for Forcing: yes

Gardeners interested in expanding their horizons will want to give snowflakes a try. Bigger in stature than their diminutive cousin the snowdrop, snowflakes grow wild in damp places in Europe and must be given a damp environment here, too, if they are to thrive. Although technically snowflakes are hardy to Zone 4 and many Zone 4 plants do well in prairie gardens, the trick, as always, is to help them survive the winter.

The genus name *Leucojum* derives from two Greek words—*leukos* (white) and *ion* (violet)—likely because *Leucojum*'s delicate fragrance compares to that of a violet.

These bulbs are endangered in the wild, so when you order bulbs, ensure that they have been grown as nursery stock.

Portrait

Although similar in appearance to the snowdrop, snowflakes differ in two ways: they are larger and they have six petals of equal length, whereas snowdrops have three short inner petals and three long outer petals. The snowflake's white, bell-shaped blossoms, which look like miniature old-fashioned lampshades, are faintly scented. Only two species, *Leucojum aestivum* and *L. vernum*, are worth trying in prairie gardens, and success is not guaranteed. The flowers of *L. vernum* are usually larger than those of *L. aestivum*.

- *Leucojum aestivum* (45 to 60 cm, 18 to 24 in.), summer snowflake, is the hardiest of the snowflakes and blooms from late spring to early summer. It produces up to eight nodding, bell-shaped flowers per stem, above glossy, dark green, grassy leaves. The six petals, which are of equal length, are white and tipped in green. 'Gravetye Giant' is a vigorous cultivar when given the conditions it prefers.
- *Leucojum vernum* (20 to 30 cm, 8 to 12 in.), spring snowflake, blooms in early spring, usually producing two nodding, bell-shaped flowers per stem, white in color with each petal tipped in green. The strappy foliage is erect, dark green, and glossy. *L. v.* var. *carpathicum* produces flowers with white petals tipped in yellow.

Where to Grow
Snowflakes are large enough to grow at the front of a perennial or shrub border, but small enough to look at home in a rock garden planting scheme. Because they inhabit wet sites in their native Europe, they look natural planted at the edge of a pond or in a bog garden. They also look smart underplanting deciduous trees and shrubs.

Perfect Partners
The spring snowflake can be combined with other early-flowering bulbs, such as snowdrops (*Galanthus* spp.), squill (*Scilla* spp.), striped squill (*Puschkinia scilloides*), and glory-of-the-snow (*Chionodoxa luciliae*), and early perennials, such as primula and hepatica. The summer snowflake looks good combined with *Camassia* and some fritillaries, which bloom at about the same time, and late-spring perennials, including three-flowered avens (*Geum triflorum*), leopard's bane (*Doronicum* spp.), and bleeding heart (*Dicentra* spp.). Snowflakes growing through a groundcover such as foamflower (*Tiarella* spp.) also paint a lovely portrait.

Ornithogalum
(or-nih-*thog*-al-um)
star-of-Bethlehem, dove's dung

PLANT AT A GLANCE (photo p. 148)

Type: true bulb
Flowering Time: mid to late spring
Height: 30 to 76 cm (12 to 30 in.)
Soil: sandy, fertile, well drained; moist during
    active growth, moderately dry after
    blooming and foliage die-back
Light: full to part sun
When to Plant: fall
How to Plant: 5 cm (2 in.) deep, 10 cm (4 in.)
    apart; 5 or 6 bulbs in a 15-cm (6-in.) pot
Propagation: division, offsets, seed
Poisonous: yes, bulbs and flowers harmful
    when ingested
Deer/Rodent Resistant: yes
Good for Forcing: no

Leucojum aestivum 'Gravetye Giant'
(snowflake) (see p. 146).
Dugald Cameron, Gardenimport

Ornithogalum is a cheerful little spring bloomer native to Europe, Asia, and North Africa, and now also naturalized in the northeastern United States and southeastern Canada. Thought to resemble a white bird, possibly a dove, this plant's botanical name derives from two Greek words—*ornis* (bird) and *gala* (milk). Some say the bulbs of *Ornithogalum umbellatum* are the "dove's dung" of the Bible, which was sold during the siege of Babylon.

The species *Ornithogalum umbellatum* was the inspiration for this plant's common name, star-of-Bethlehem, because its delightful star-shaped flowers brighten the dry, rocky hillsides around Bethlehem. Another species, *O. thyrsoides*, has the tongue-twisting common name of chincherinchee in South Africa. This sound apparently results when you rub your thumb and forefinger tightly up and down its stem.

The Greeks used to eat the shoots of some *Ornithogalum* species as we would eat asparagus today.

Portrait

Ornithogalum umbellatum is the star-of-Bethlehem species with a proven track record in some prairie gardens. Its linear, medium green basal leaves are veined white below and have a central white stripe on the surface. The reverse is true for the white, star-shaped flowers, which have a central green stripe on the undersides of petals. Flowering stems produce from six to twenty blossoms, each attached by a long stalk. Blossoms are

Ornithogalum umbellatum (star-of-Bethlehem). *Ken*

long lasting, despite the fact that they open in the morning and close again at the end of each day.

Where to Grow
Plant star-of-Bethlehem at the front of sunny borders, in rock gardens, or in containers.

Perfect Partners
White-flowered star-of-Bethlehem is an attractive addition to blue-and-yellow plantings that might include blue grape hyacinth (*Muscari* spp.), yellow leopard's bane (*Doronicum* spp.), *Euphorbia polychroma*, and mid-season narcissus. It is also lovely combined with mid-season tulips (*Tulipa*) of any color and brilliant orange avens (*Geum coccineum*).

Oxalis
(ox-*al*-iss)
wood sorrel, shamrock

PLANT AT A GLANCE (photo this page)

Oxalis adenophylla (wood sorrel). Ken Girard

Type: true bulb, tuber, or rhizome, depending on species
Flowering Time: early summer (*Oxalis adenophylla*), early to late summer (*O. regnellii*, *O. tetraphylla*)
Height: 10 to 15 cm (4 to 6 in.)
Soil: average to fertile, moist, well drained
Light: full sun to light shade
When to Plant: fall (*Oxalis adenophylla*), late spring (*O. regnellii*, *O. tetraphylla*)
How to Plant: 5 cm (2 in.) deep, 10 cm (4 in.) apart
Propagation: division, offsets, seed
Poisonous: no
Deer/Rodent Resistant: yes
Good for Forcing: yes, *Oxalis adenophylla* only

The genus *Oxalis* includes many bulbous, tuberous, and rhizomatous plants that feature cloverlike foliage and dainty, funnel- to cup-shaped flowers. Some of these pretty pink- or white-flowering plants are sold as Irish shamrocks, notably around St. Patrick's Day; in Ireland, however, the name "shamrock" (derived from an Irish word for clover, *seamróg*) is more commonly applied to several *Trifolium* species, members of the clover family.

Because most of the desirable ornamental *Oxalis* species originate from South Africa or Central and South America, they must be grown as tender bulbs or houseplants—with one exception. *O. adenophylla*, which hails from high elevations in Argentina and Chile, is hardy to at least -29° C (-20° F), and it has been overwintered successfully with protection in prairie gardens.

Portrait
Oxalis adenophylla (10 cm, 4 in.) produces attractive mound-forming, gray-green leaves composed of many heart-shaped leaflets. The solitary, five-petalled, lavender pink flowers are veined with darker pink and have maroon eyes. They are held above the compact foliage on thin, wiry stems.

The only real limitation on growing tender *Oxalis* species as annuals is availability. Two generally available species are notable for their striking foliage. *O. tetraphylla* (syn. *O. deppei*) (15 cm, 6 in.), good luck plant or lucky clover, is a popular Mexican species with reddish purple flowers and cloverlike leaves composed of four lobed leaflets, each leaflet marked with reddish brown at the base. The cultivar 'Iron Cross' has dark purple leaf markings that form a distinctive cross; 'Alba' is a white-flowered cultivar.

Oxalis regnellii 'Triangularis' (15 cm, 6 in.), red velvet shamrock, has eye-catching deep maroon purple, triangular leaflets with a flare of violet pink at the base of each. Dainty, lilac pink flowers are held above the mounded foliage.

Where to Grow
The neat foliage and dainty blooms of all *Oxalis* species make them delightful additions to any rock garden. They are also good choices for the front of a border or as a tidy edging for pathways. The intriguing foliage and showy flowers of these plants are also shown to fine advantage in container plantings, including hanging baskets.

Perfect Partners
Accompany *Oxalis* in the rock garden or border with low-growing perennials such as creeping phlox, dwarf irises, dianthus, *Primula auricula*, and creeping thyme (*Thymus* spp.). Use your imagination to create lovely container plantings by combining *Oxalis* with annual companions. *Helichrysum petiolare* 'Limelight' or 'Licorice', sweet alyssum (*Lobularia maritima*), bacopa, and sweet potato vine (*Ipomoea batatus*) are just a few suggestions.

Triteleia

(treye-*tell*-ee-uh)
triteleia, grass nut

PLANT AT A GLANCE (photo p. 152)

Type: corm
Flowering Time: mid-summer
Height: 60 cm (24 in.)
Soil: average to fertile, well drained
Light: full sun
When to Plant: fall; alternatively, store bulbs in a cool, dry place for the winter and plant out in early spring
How to Plant: 8 to 13 cm (3 to 5 in.) deep, 8 cm (3 in.) apart
Propagation: division, offsets, seed; separate small cormels when plant is dormant, but only infrequently as triteleias dislike disturbance
Poisonous: no
Deer/Rodent Resistant: no
Good for Forcing: no

Somewhat amazingly, two patches of *Triteleia laxa* 'Queen Fabiola' have managed to thrive for three years in one of the co-authors' Calgary garden, blooming more prolifically each summer. Like other triteleias, 'Queen Fabiola' flowers bloom when all the other spring-flowering bulbs are but fading memories, making its umbels of deep blue-purple flowers a pleasant surprise in July.

Triteleia may be familiar to some gardeners as *Brodiaea*, and it is still frequently sold under that name. Many of the original members of the genus *Brodiaea* have been reassigned to *Triteleia* or *Dichelostemma*, but since most of these plants won't grow on the prairies, this is of academic interest only.

Portrait

Triteleia laxa 'Queen Fabiola' is the best and most commonly available triteleia for garden use. It bears large, loose umbels of up to twenty-five rich blue-purple, funnel-shaped flowers that are about 5 cm (2 in.) long. The grassy basal leaves die back around blooming time.

Triteleia laxa is native to the grasslands and open pine forests of California and Oregon and is adapted to hot, dry summers. It does best in a sunny, sheltered location with excellent drainage, where it receives spring moisture. It is essential to protect the corms with an 8-cm (3-in.) or deeper layer of organic mulch if you want them to survive the winter, particularly in the Chinook Zone where snow cover is unreliable.

Triteleia laxa 'Queen Fabiola' (triteleia, grass nut).
Lesley Reynolds

'Queen Fabiola' has a lazy wildflower charm that suits a natural grassland setting, provided it is not too windswept. However, it would also be right at home in a sunny, informal perennial border or a cottage-style garden. 'Queen Fabiola' is also delightful in flower arrangements and is a fine addition to a cutting garden.

Perfect Partners

In a wildflower garden, plant 'Queen Fabiola' with drought-tolerant native plants, such as gaillardia, liatris, wild blue flax (*Linum lewisii*), or yellow prairie coneflower (*Ratibida columnifera*). Good companions in the perennial border include alliums, feverfew (*Tanacetum parthenium*), spike speedwell (*Veronica spicata*), monarda, and lavender (*Lavandula*).

Tender Bulbs

Gardeners who love brilliant, unusual, and exotic flowers need look no further than the tender bulb section of their favorite catalogues. These are the southerners, and with the notable exception of the begonia, they love the mid-summer heat. Although there are many lovely summer-flowering bulbs available, four stellar performers will be highlighted here. Begonia, canna, dahlia, and gladiola are justifiably the most popular tender bulbs in prairie gardens; they are easy to grow and widely available in an impressive array of colors and sizes. In addition to detailed entries about these "big four," a chart of other delightful, but often more temperamental, tender bulbs has been included. These plants are usually best treated as annuals, but the bulbs may be saved from year to year (see Chapter 6, p. 54, Lifting and Storing Tender Bulbs).

The growing techniques and timing for tender bulbs are similar to those for growing annuals. Although tender bulbs can be planted directly outdoors when the soil is warm, blooming is more likely to be successful if they are given a head start indoors or in a greenhouse. Most tender bulbs should be started indoors six weeks before the last expected frost date, with the exception of begonias and calla lilies (*Zantedeschia*), which should be started approximately three months before the last expected frost date. The bloom time of tender bulbs is largely dependent upon

Tender Bulbs

Botanical Name	Common Name	LIGHT			HEIGHT				COLOR							BLOOM SEASON				FEATURES				TYPE						PLANTING DEPTH				
		Full sun	Part sun	Light shade	<30 cm (>12 in.)	30-60 cm (12-24 in.)	60-90 cm (24-36 in.)	>90 cm (<36 in.)	White	Yellow	Orange	Red	Pink	Purple	Blue	Early summer	Mid-summer	Late summer	Fall	Fragrant	Variegated foliage	Poisonous	Deer/Rodent Resistant	True bulb	Corm	Tuber	Rhizome	Tuberous root	Bulb neck at soil level	.5 cm (1/4 in.)	2.5-5 cm (1-2 in.)	7.5-10 cm (3-4 in.)	12.5-15 cm (5-6 in.)	17.5-30 cm (7-12 in.)
Agapanthus	Lily-of-the-Nile	•	•				•	•	•						•				•			•					•				•			
Alstroemeria	Peruvian lily	•	•				•	•	•	•	•		•	•				•				•						•					•	
Babiana	Baboon flower	•			•				•	•				•	•			•		•					•								•	
Begonia	Tuberous begonia		•	•	•	•			•	•	•	•	•			•	•	•								•				•				
Caladium	Fancy-leaved caladium		•	•	•	•			•			•	•								•					•					•			
Canna	Canna	•					•	•	•	•	•	•	•				•	•			•						•				•			
Crinum	Crinum lily	•	•				•	•	•				•					•		•		•	•	•					•					•
Crocosmia	Montbretia	•				•	•			•	•	•					•	•							•							•		
Dahlia	Dahlia	•				•	•		•	•	•	•	•	•			•	•	•				•					•				•		
Eucomis	Pineapple flower	•	•			•			•					•				•		•				•								•		
Freesia	Freesia	•	•			•			•	•	•	•	•	•			•	•		•					•						•			
Galtonia	Summer hyacinth	•					•		•									•		•				•								•		
Gladiolus	Gladiola	•					•	•	•	•	•	•	•	•			•	•					•		•							•		
Hymenocallis	Spider lily	•	•			•			•	•								•		•		•	•	•					•					
Nerine	Guernsey lily	•				•			•			•	•						•				•	•								•		
Ranunculus	Persian buttercup	•	•		•				•	•	•	•	•			•						•	•			•					•			
Sparaxis	Harlequin flower	•			•	•			•	•	•	•	•	•			•	•					•		•						•			
Tigridia	Tiger flower	•				•			•	•	•	•	•					•						•								•		
Tritonia	Flame freesia	•				•	•		•	•	•	•	•					•							•						•			
Watsonia	Bugle lily	•					•	•	•	•	•	•	•					•				•			•		•						•	
Zantedeschia	Calla lily		•	•		•	•		•	•	•	•	•	•			•	•				•	•				•				•			
Zephyranthes	Fairy lily	•			•				•	•			•					•					•	•							•			

Refer to this chart for descriptive and cultural information about many tender bulbs that are widely available in garden centers and well-known mail order catalogues.

when they are planted, whether they are started indoors or planted directly in the garden, and the amount of heat they receive. If temperatures dip too low—a distinct possibility during an average prairie summer—some of these sulky beauties will simply refuse to bloom. Plant them in the warmest, most sheltered areas of the garden, or be prepared to move container-grown bulbs indoors temporarily during chilly weather.

Begonia

(bee-*goh*-nyah)
tuberous begonia

PLANT AT A GLANCE (photos p. 156)

Type: tuber
Flowering Time: early to late summer
Height: 20 to 45 cm (8 to 18 in.)
Soil: fertile, moist, well drained
Light: part sun to light shade
When to Plant: indoors in late winter, two to three months before the last expected frost date, move outdoors after the last expected frost date
How to Plant: tubers should be planted just slightly below the soil surface, indented side up; 23 to 30 cm (9 to 12 in.) apart in flowerbeds, three or four tubers per hanging basket or pot
Propagation: division, cuttings, seed
Poisonous: no
Deer/Rodent Resistant: no
Good for Forcing: no

The voluptuous blooms of tuberous begonias are long-standing favorites in prairie gardens. No other summer-flowering bulb offers such a huge variety of spectacular colors and flower forms or as long a bloom period.

The genus *Begonia* comprises over fifteen hundred species, some fibrous rooted, some rhizomatous, and some tuberous. Begonias were discovered in the West Indies in 1690 by a French monk, Charles Plumier, who named them after a French colonial official, Michel Bégon. Unfortunately, since there were two late seventeenth-century officials by this name, one a governor of Santo Domingo and the other an Intendant of French Canada, the exact identity of the Bégon of begonia fame is unclear. The exotic blooms of tuberous begonias (*Begonia* x *tuberhybrida*) reveal their tropical and subtropical ancestry. Modern hybridized begonias descend from about eight South American species collected in the mid-nineteenth century by plant-hunter and explorer Richard Pearce, who was employed by the notable English nursery James Veitch and Sons of Chelsea. Many of these species, all single flowered, grew in cool but frost-free habitats at altitudes of 3,000 m (10,000 ft.) in Chile, Ecuador, Peru, and Bolivia. Unfortunately, Pearce succumbed to yellow fever at the tender age of 30 on a subsequent plant-hunting expedition to Panama in 1867.

The first tuberous begonia hybrid was produced in 1869 by John Seden, the foreman at James Veitch and Sons. Many other hybrids followed as the enthusiasm for this fashionable new plant reached a fever pitch. To satisfy the demand, both nurserymen and amateur plant growers contributed to the development of many new varieties. The most famous begonia producer, Blackmore and Langdon, was a collaboration of Charles Langdon and James Blackmore, passionate begonia enthusiasts and hybridists who joined forces in 1900, and was responsible for hundreds of begonia introductions. Begonias were also widely grown and hybridized in Belgium, France, the United States, and Scotland. Currently, most begonia tubers come from Belgian growers in the Ghent/Lochrist area, or from California.

Portrait

Tuberous begonia flowers can be white, pink, salmon, rose, yellow, apricot, scarlet, red, or orange—in fact, almost every color but blue. Many different flower forms have been developed, and tuberous begonias may be classified into several rather loosely defined groups. The list below includes the most popular and readily available types.

- Multiflora begonias (15 to 25 cm, 6 to 10 in.) are compact with single, semi, or fully double flowers up to 10 cm (4 in.) wide, produced over a long blooming season.
- Non-Stop begonias (15 to 25 cm, 6 to 10 in.) are hybrids of Multifloras and large double-flowered begonias. The double, 10-cm (4-in.) flowers are produced in abundance all summer long, and are among the most heat tolerant of the tuberous begonias. Colors in the Non-Stop Series include apricot, apple

---

Tips for Growing Begonias

Begonias can be fussy, but they are well worth the effort. Here are a few tips for growing beautiful begonias.

- Avoid planting begonias in windy areas, but do provide good air circulation.
- Plant begonias where they will receive bright light, but not direct sun. They will not perform well in dense shade.
- Begonias are at their best in cooler summer temperatures, so plant them away from areas that tend to be heat traps.
- Although begonias enjoy a humid environment, avoid wetting the leaves when watering.
- The leaves and flowers on a begonia plant all face one way, so be sure to position them correctly when planting.
- Fertilize begonias with a half-strength flowering plant fertilizer (e.g., 15-30-15) every two weeks during active growth.
- To encourage larger blooms, pinch off the small side buds (female flowers) under the bigger, showier male flowers.
- Stop fertilizing as flower production slows in late summer.
- Withhold water when leaves begin to turn yellow.
- Lift tubers, clean them, and store indoors in a cool dry place (see Chapter 6, p. 54, Lifting and Storing Tender Bulbs.)

Begonia Pendula type. *Lesley Reynolds*

Begonia Non-Stop Series, *B. semperflorens* (wax begonia, fibrous-rooted begonia). *Liesbeth Leatherbarrow*

blossom, copper, rose pink, white, yellow, salmon, scarlet, orange, and a white and pink bicolor.

- Large-flowered double begonias (30 to 60 cm, 12 to 24 in.) are a large group that includes camellia, rose, and carnation flower forms. The gorgeous, brightly colored blooms are often frilled or ruffled, and can measure up to 18 cm (7 in.) across. There are hundreds of cultivars and the selection will vary from year to year; however, some outstanding cultivars are 'Billie Langdon' (white), 'City of Ballaarat' (orange), 'Falstaff' (rose pink), 'Primrose' (yellow), 'Roy Hartley' (salmon rose), 'Sugar Candy' (pale pink), and 'Zulu' (red).
- Picotee and bicolor begonias (20 to 30 cm, 8 to 12 in.) are types of large-flowered double begonias that bear two-toned flowers. Picotee begonias are usually yellow or white with a narrow pink or red edging around the petals. 'Can Can' (yellow with red edges), 'Fairylight' (white with red edges), and 'Fred Martin' (cream with red edges) are lovely classic picotee begonias. Bicolor begonias have a wider rim of color around the edge of each petal.
- Pendula begonias are trailing varieties, superb for hanging baskets, window boxes, or tall urns or pots where their cascading habit shows to best advantage. Older varieties of pendulas had small, starry flowers, but more recent cultivars, such as the Cascade Series, bear white, yellow, red, or pink double flowers up to 8 cm (3 in.) across. The Illumination Series of pendula begonias produces pink or orange flowers and is slightly more heat tolerant. There are also picotee pendula begonias.

Where to Grow
Begonias are superb plants for all types of containers, including hanging baskets, planters, and window boxes. Upright, compact varieties, such as those in the Non-Stop Series, are also suitable bedding plants for a lightly shaded area or a bed that receives only morning or evening sun.

Perfect Partners
Generally speaking, begonias look best on their own or with other begonias. However, they do look handsome in a hanging basket with shade-tolerant, trailing foliage plants such as ivy (*Hedera* spp.) or periwinkle (*Vinca* spp.). Select companions that will complement, not compete with, the large and showy begonia blooms. Small-flowered annuals such as lobelia, nemesia, and impatiens, and fibrous-rooted wax begonias (*Begonia semperflorens*) are good choices.

Canna
(*kah*-nah)
canna

PLANT AT A GLANCE (photos p. 160)

Type: rhizome
Flowering Time: late summer to early fall
Height: 0.6 to 2 m (2 to 6.5 ft.)
Soil: fertile, moist, well drained
Light: full sun
When to Plant: spring; indoors in pots, six weeks before last expected frost date, move outside after last expected frost date; outdoors, one to two weeks before last expected frost date
How to Plant: 2.5 cm (1 in.) deep, 30 cm (12 in.) apart; in fall, bring potted bulbs or those dug up from the garden indoors and store in a cool, dry, dark place
Propagation: division
Poisonous: no
Deer/Rodent Resistant: no
Good for Forcing: no

For lovers of "bold"—bold color, bold form, bold size—exotic-looking cannas add an element of excitement and adventure to the landscape. They thrive in areas with warm days and nights, making all except Chinook Zone prairie gardens a perfect setting for their conspicuous beauty.

Traditional cannas, with their spikes of scarlet red flowers and distinctive bronze or green foliage the size of banana tree leaves, became popular as graveyard plantings in the mid-twentieth century. As a result they quickly fell out of favor among home gardeners, but plant-breeding wizards soon put an end to that sorry trend. Today's hybrids produce foliage with such a wide range in color and variegation, and flowers in both hot and pastel shades, that they have regained their popularity.

The name *Canna* comes from the Greek *kanna*, which means reed-like. This likely describes the tall, thin flower stalks that shoot up from ground level.

Portrait

Canna flowers, which are borne at the ends of long, thin flower stalks, are asymmetric. Similar in appearance to gladiolas, each has three petals forming a tube at their base, three sepals, and five prominent stamens that also look like petals. The flowers, which are hummingbird magnets, come in hot, vibrant shades of red, orange, and yellow, or pastel shades of cream, rose, and apricot. Whereas the flower size of older cultivars is disproportionately small compared to the rest of the plant, new introductions have much larger and showier blossoms. To promote continuous bloom, deadhead conscientiously. New flower stalks will develop just below where spent flowers have been removed.

Canna foliage is theatrical, both because of its impressive size and the unique coloration that has been introduced in recent years. Broad, individual, paddle-shaped leaves range in length from 30 cm (12 in.) to more than 60 cm (24 in.) and alternate on the stems; they are sheathed at the bottom and unfurl slowly, revealing the reedlike flower stems that grow up from the crown at ground level, through their interior.

Though traditional cannas can grow to 1.8 m (6 ft.) or taller, two shorter series are better suited to the average urban garden. The Opera Series cannas reach a height of 1.2 m (4 ft.) and the Pfitzer Series, of which 'Pfitzer's Chinese Coral' and 'Pfitzer's Primrose Yellow' are two examples, are less than 90 cm (36 in.) tall. Dozens of other hybrids are also available for gardeners, and they can be loosely grouped according to their foliage color—green, bronze-burgundy, or variegated.

- Green foliage: 'Aida' (baby pink, short), 'Jester' (red flowers fringed with yellow, short), 'The President' (red flowers, tall), 'Richard Wallace' (yellow flowers, short), 'Madame Butterfly' (yellowish pink flowers, short)
- Bronze-burgundy foliage: 'Black Knight' (deep red flowers, burgundy foliage, tall), 'Dawn Pink' (coral flowers, bronze foliage, short), 'Freedom Pink' (self-cleaning pink flowers, burgundy foliage, short), 'Red King Humbert' (red flowers, bronze foliage, tall)

- Variegated foliage: 'Pink Sunburst' (pink flowers, foliage variegated purple, pink, and gold, short), 'Pretoria' (orange flowers, foliage variegated green with yellow, short), 'Striped Beauty' (yellow flowers, foliage variegated green and yellow, short), 'Tropicana' (orange flowers, foliage variegated red, pink, yellow, and green, tall)

Where to Grow

Tall canna varieties make a bold, tropical statement at the back of large mixed borders. Where space permits, a mass planting of cannas in a bed of their own adds drama to the landscape. Cannas of all sizes also serve admirably as a temporary hedge, whereas dwarf cannas make good container plants and are welcome additions to average-sized flowerbeds.

Perfect Partners

Because cannas are vibrantly colored, they look best when surrounded by simple foliage plants. Ornamental grasses make good partners, especially mid-sized, non-variegated ones such as blue oat grass (*Helictotrichon sempervirens*) and purple moor grass (*Molinia caerulea*). Low-growing shrubs such as spirea, dogwood (*Cornus* spp.), and 'Polar Bear' willow (*Salix silicola* 'Polar Bear') also set the tropical foliage off to advantage. Juniper (*Juniperus*) and cedar (*Thuja*) provide an elegant evergreen backdrop to most types of cannas.

Dahlia
(*dah*-lee-ah, *day*-lee-ah)
dahlia

PLANT AT A GLANCE (photo p. 161)

Type: tuberous root
Flowering Time: mid-summer to fall
Height: 0.3 to 2.0 m (1 to 6.5 ft.)
Soil: fertile, moist, well drained
Light: full sun
When to Plant: spring; indoors in pots, six weeks before the last expected frost date, move outside after last expected frost date; outdoors, one to two weeks before the last expected frost date
How to Plant: see sidebar
Propagation: division, cuttings, seed
Poisonous: no
Deer/Rodent Resistant: yes
Good for Forcing: no

For dahlia lovers, the only word to describe the plant of their affections is dazzling! From the pint-size Mignon types with 5-cm (2-in.) flowerheads to the enormous Giant types with flowerheads at least 25 cm (10 in.) across, the array of available dahlia cultivars is a collector's dream come true. Over twenty thousand dahlia cultivars have been developed since mild "Dahliamania" swept Europe in the mid-1800s; amazingly, plant breeders have worked their magic from only three main parent species—*Dahlia coccinea*, *D. pinnata*, and *D. hortensis*.

Native to Mexico, dahlias were cultivated by the Aztecs for their fleshy tuberous roots, as an important source of food and medicinal ingredients. The hollow stems of the towering *Dahlia imperialis* (9 m, 30 ft.) were also indispensable to the Aztecs who used them as piping to move precious water from the mountains to their villages. In fact, the Aztec word for dahlia, *cocoxochitl*, means water pipe.

Cocoxochitl were first introduced into European culture via Spain in 1789, but plant collectors also sent seed to plant breeders in Berlin and Paris, and by 1815, all the familiar shapes and colors of modern dahlias, except for cactus-types, had been developed. Along the way, this versatile plant was named "dahlia" in honor of Anders Dahl, a Swedish botanist who developed many popular cultivars.

Portrait

Dahlias are members of the *Asteraceae* or daisy family and, as such, produce flower heads that consist of single or multiple rows of petal-like ray florets surrounding a central cluster of smaller, tubular disk florets. The flower heads, which come in every color but blue and true green and

Canna 'Madame Butterfly' (see p. 157). *Lesley Rey*

Canna foliage, variegated green and yellow (see p. 157). *Liesbeth Leatherbarrow*

always turn to face the light, are held high on straight, somewhat brittle, hollow stems clothed in medium to dark green leaves. Individual leaves are divided into leaflets with toothed margins and rounded tips; their size varies proportionately with cultivar size —the bigger the cultivar, the bigger the leaf.

Because so many different dahlia cultivars are available, and because dahlia shows are popular among aficionados, a formal classification system was developed to help describe and keep track of the differences.

Dahlia 'Garden Pride'. *Liesbeth Leatherbarrow*

The first level of classification is based on bloom diameter.

- Mignon - 5 cm (2 in.)
- Miniature (M) - 5 to 10 cm (2 to 4 in.)
- Small (BB) - 10 to 15 cm (4 to 6 in.)
- Medium (B) - 15 to 20 cm (6 to 8 in.)
- Large (A) - 20 to 25 cm (8 to 10 in.)
- Giant (AA) - greater than 25 cm (10 in.)

A second level of classification is based on flower head shape. This classification is a useful guide, but is not applied rigidly by local dahlia societies, which often make adjustments to accommodate their own needs and traditions.

I. Single-flowered dahlias (30 cm, 12 in.) produce a single flat row of ray florets that is arranged around central disk florets. Try 'Sneezy' (white) or 'Sweetheart' (pink and white with big yellow centers).

II. Anemone-flowered dahlias (60 to 90 cm, 24 to 36 in.) produce one or more rows of ray florets around a dense central cluster of disk florets that resembles a pincushion.

III. Collarettes (up to 1.2 m, 4 ft.) consist of one row of ray florets surrounding a second row of shorter ray florets that form a collar around central disk florets. 'Alden Cherub' (white) and 'Wheels' (red and yellow) are good examples of collarettes.

IV.   Waterlily dahlias (90 cm, 36 in.) look like waterlilies; they are fully double and consist of rows of broad, flat, or slightly upwardly curved ray florets. Try 'Lisa' (lavender and white) or 'Angel's Wings' (light pink).

V.   Formal Decorative dahlias (0.9 to 2 m, 3 to 6.5 ft.) are fully double, with rows of flat ray florets with rounded or pointed tips, curved slightly downward towards the stem; they are arranged in a regular fashion around the center, although there are no central disk florets. Try 'Heat Wave' (yellow and red) or 'Splish Splash' (purple and white).

VI.   Informal Decorative dahlias (0.9 to 2.0 m, 3 to 6 ft.) are fully double, with rows of long twisted or pointed ray florets arranged in an irregular fashion around the center; there are no central disk florets. 'Chilson's Pride' (pink), 'Kasuga' (apple blossom pink), and 'Dark Magic' (fuchsia) are interesting choices.

VII.   Ball dahlias (90 cm, 36 in.) have ball-shaped flower heads that consist of rows of blunt-tipped ray florets, with their margins curled inward for at least half their length; there are no central disk florets. Try 'Cornell' (red) or 'Eveline' (ivory tinged with lilac).

VIII.   Pompom dahlias (60 to 90 cm, 24 to 36 in.) produce ball-shaped flowerheads that consist of rows of ray florets that are blunt-tipped with the margins curled inward for their entire length; there are no central disk florets. Two good choices are 'Chick-A-Dee' (red and white) and 'Mark Lockwood' (dark lavender).

IX.   Cactus-flowered dahlias (1.2 m, 4 ft.) consist of rows of elongated ray florets, with their margins tightly curled downward for more than half their length, giving them a quill shape. 'Light Touch' (purple and white) and 'Camano Messenger' (pink and yellow) are good examples.

X.   Semi-cactus-flowered dahlias (1.2 m, 4 ft.) produce rows of elongated ray florets with a broad base, with their margins tightly curled downward for less than half their length. 'Rip City' (dark red), 'Show-N-Tell' (red and yellow), and 'Vanquisher' (lavender and white) are interesting possibilities.

XI.   Peony-flowered dahlias (90 cm, 36 in.) have two or more rows of flat, broad ray florets around a central cluster of disk florets; the ray florets closest to the center may be twisted. 'Bishop of Llandaff' (black-red foliage, dark red blooms) is one of the best known peony-flowered dahlias.

XII.   Fimbriated dahlias (90 cm, 36 in.) are fully double, with no central disk; their ray florets are split and twisted for part of their length, giving a fringed or "fimbriated" effect. 'Harmony' (pink and yellow) and 'Nenekazi' (red and pink) are two examples of these dahlias.

XIII.   Miscellaneous includes all other dahlias that don't fit into the previous eleven categories.

Where to Grow

Short dahlias with relatively small flowerheads are excellent for including as accents in low-growing borders or as container plants. They are most effective when massed in groups of three or five plants of the same cultivar. Taller dahlias make striking accents towards the back of mixed and perennial borders; they can also be used as temporary screens or hedges. Always choose planting spots sheltered from the wind, since dahlias' hollow stems are brittle and break relatively easily.

Tips for Growing Dahlias

- Plant in areas sheltered from the wind, away from trees and shrubs that will compete for nutrients.
- Plant outdoors about one week before the last predicted frost date.
- For dahlias taller than 1.2 m (4 ft.), space 1.2 to 1.5 m (4 to 5 ft.) apart; for dahlias smaller than 1.2 m (4 ft.), space 30 to 60 cm (12 to 24 in.) apart.
- For short dahlias, plant about 10 cm (4 in.) deep, with compost and bulb fertilizer in the bottom of the hole, separated by a layer of playbox sand. Fill hole with soil and water; don't water again until shoots emerge.
- For tall dahlias, use the "deep planting method" to provide stability as the plant grows taller. Dig a hole 30 cm (12 in.) deep and 30 to 45 cm (12 to 18 in.) across, mix compost and bulb fertilizer into the soil at the bottom of the hole, and cover with a layer of playbox sand. Place the tuberous roots horizontally in the bottom of the hole, with stem buds pointing upward. Cover the roots with about 8 cm (3 in.) of soil, water, and don't water again until shoots emerge. Gradually fill in the hole as the shoots grow, much as you would for growing leeks.
- Add a stake at planting time for tall dahlias, about 15 cm (6 in.) shorter than the mature height of the plant.
- To make short dahlias bushier, pinch the growing tip after the first three sets of leaves have formed, then again after the next three sets have formed; this will encourage side shoots to develop.
- To grow the largest flowers possible, remove at an early stage all of the buds (disbud) except one at the end of the stem.
- Water and fertilize regularly during the growing season, using a fertilizer with low nitrogen (small first number); otherwise, you will have lush foliage at the expense of large or numerous blossoms.
- After the first frost, lift dahlia roots and let them dry. Then remove dry soil and store them indoors in dry sand, peat moss, or vermiculite, in a cool, dark, dry place for the winter.
- Divide in fall or spring and replant outdoors the following spring. Note that dahlia buds or "eyes" are found at the base of the stem, so when dividing, make sure that each division includes a portion of the stem with an associated bud.

Grandiflorus *Gladiolus* x *hortulanus* (gladiola) (see p. 165). *Liesbeth Leatherbarrow*

Perfect Partners

If you are growing dahlias for show, plant them on their own, in separate rows, where they are not in competition with other plants. Tall dahlias planted in perennial and mixed borders look fine grouped with globe thistle (*Echinops* spp.), bee balm (*Monarda* spp.), garden phlox (*Phlox paniculata*), lilies, and tall ornamental grasses. Shorter dahlia cultivars are delightful in combination with 'Sunny Border Blue' veronica, 'Butterfly Blue' scabiosa, and daylilies (*Hemerocallis* spp.).

Gladiolus

(gla-dee-*oh*-luss)
gladiola, sword lily

PLANT AT A GLANCE
(photos pp. 29, 164, this page)

Type: corm

Gladiolus callianthus (peacock orchid).
Lesley Reynolds

Tips for Growing Gladiolas

- If possible, choose corms that are taller than they are wide; broad, flat corms are more mature and less vigorous.
- Plant 8 to 15 cm (3 to 6 in.) deep, and 8 to 15 cm (3 to 6 in.) apart in spring; cover with only a few centimeters of soil at first, gradually adding more soil as the plants grow, until the planting hole is full.
- Plant tall varieties even deeper, to give stems extra strength. Hilling the soil (drawing the soil up around the base of the plant) to about 15 cm (6 in.) around the growing stem will also help prevent the gladiolas from leaning when they are

in flower.
- Very tall varieties should be planted in sheltered spots or supported with stakes in windy spots.
- Make successive plantings to extend bloom season, in addition to planting early- and late-blooming varieties.
- Plant gladiolas in a new location each year to help prevent the spread of disease.
- Most gladiola hybrids bloom from sixty to one hundred days after planting, depending on the cultivar; the warmer the weather the sooner they bloom.
- Cut flower spikes when the first buds at the base show color and begin to open.

- When cutting, leave four or five leaves on the plant to manufacture the food for next year's blooms.
- For gladiolas planted to bloom in the garden, deadhead the entire flower stalk after the last blossoms have faded.
- Tiny insects called thrips can attack late-blooming gladiolas, distorting blossoms and streaking foliage; use a chemical treatment during growth and storage to deal with the problem.
- In fall, bring potted corms or those dug up from the garden indoors and store in a cool, dry, dark place.

Flowering Time: mid to late summer
Height: 0.5 to 1.8 m (1.5 to 6 ft.)
Soil: fertile, well drained; keep moist during active growth, moderately dry after blooming and foliage die-back
Light: full to part sun
When to Plant: spring; indoors in pots, six weeks before last expected frost date, move outside after last expected frost date; outdoors, one to two weeks before last expected frost date
How to Plant: see sidebar
Propagation: division, offsets, seed
Deer/Rodent Resistant: no
Good for Forcing: no

When it comes to gladiolas, gardeners have strong feelings—they either love them or they don't. It is virtually impossible to be neutral about these aristocrats of the plant world, but considering that gladiolas are the second most popular cut flower in North America, tucked in neatly after roses on the score card, the balance is clearly tipped in their favor.

Love them or not, gladiolas make valuable vertical accents in prairie gardens. Their botanical name is identical to the Latin word for small sword—*gladiolus*—in reference to its short, bladelike, spiky foliage. Not surprisingly, its common name is sword lily. Gladiolas at one time also answered to the name *Xiphium*, an ancient Greek word for sword.

Like the mythical origins of so many plants, gladiolas were also the result of spilt blood—in this case, the blood of an innocent man in the wrong place at the wrong time. Erisichthon did not believe in the Goddess Ceres and repeatedly ransacked her sacred grove of trees. When a worshipper tried to stop him, Erisichthon beheaded him, and Ceres caused little sword-shaped plants to spring from the droplets of blood, which she called *gladiolus*.

Most, though not all, gladiolas come from South Africa where their corms, said to have the taste of chestnuts, were an important food source. A few species also originated in the Holy Land, and are thought to be the "lilies of the field" that Jesus referred to in his Sermon on the Mount.

Although some species gladiolas can be ordered through specialty catalogues, by far the most popular gladiolas are hybrids, *Gladiolus* x *hortulanus*, of which there are more than ten thousand on record. Because of their great complexity, gladiolas are variously classified on the basis of flower size, color, shape, and form. Not surprisingly, there are almost as many classifications as there are gladiola societies.

Portrait

Gladiolas produce dramatic, showy flower spikes of funnel-shaped, sometimes frilly flowers that each have six segments: one central upper segment, three smaller lower segments, and two quite large segments, one on each side. The stemless blossoms, which come in all colors except true delphinium blue, may be arranged in pairs, directly opposite each other on the stem (formally) or one above the other (informally), all facing the same direction. Individual blossoms last only a week, opening from the bottom of the spike up, but as lower ones begin fade, new ones begin to open farther up the stem, resulting in a respectable amount of bloom time before the flower spike calls it quits. The narrow, sharp, flat leaves form a basal fan.

In terms of height, gladiolas are ranked as small (60 to 90 cm, 24 to 36 in.), medium (0.9 to 1.2 m, 3 to 4 ft.), or giant (more than 1.2 m, 4 ft.). In specialty catalogues, you may also come across a three-digit (trinomial) numerical code with each entry; it describes the hybrid in terms of blossom size and color. The first digit refers to the flower width in inches, the second refers to color (0 white, 1 yellow, 2 orange, 3 salmon, 4 pink, 5 red, 6 rose, 7 lavender, 8 violet, 9 brown or other), and the third refers to color intensity (the higher the number, the more intense the color).

One popular classification subdivides gladiolas into three main groups: Grandiflorus, Nanus, and Primulinus. Available cultivars change as often as new catalogues are issued, so only a few outstanding choices are listed in each category.

- Grandiflorus: corms produce a single spike, 35 to 90 cm (14 to 36 in.) long, with as many as twenty-eight buds (up to twelve open at a time) formally arranged on the stem. Some corms produce multiple flower spikes. They are further described according to the size of the bottom flower on the spike: giant, more than 14 cm (5.5 in.); large, 11 to 14 cm (4.5 to 5.5 in.); medium, 9 to 11 cm (3.5 to 4.5 in.); small, 6 to 9 cm (2.5 to 3.5 in.); and miniature, less than 6 cm (2.5 in.). Plants sporting miniature flowers are usually 90 cm (36 in.) tall, whereas plants sporting giants tower at 1.8 m (6 ft.). They flower from mid-summer to fall. Try 'Award' (rose pink fading to white), 'Dream's End' (pale orange with yellow centers), 'Midnight Moon' (deep blue violet with prominent creamy white markings), and 'Stardust' (pale yellow with lighter yellow throats).
- Nanus: corms produce two to three slender spikes, 23 to 35 cm (9 to 14 in.) long. Up to seven flowers (three to four open at a time) are loosely arranged on the stem. They flower in mid-summer. Try 'Amanda Mahy' (salmon pink flecked in violet and white), 'Charm' (purple red with ivory throats), 'Elvira'

(pale pink with red markings), 'Impressive' (rose pink with darker pink, diamond-shaped markings), and 'Nymph' (white with cream markings edged in red).

- Primulinus: corms produce a single stem, 30 to 60 cm (12 to 24 in.) long, with up to twenty buds (up to seven open at a time) informally arranged on the stem. The top flower segment is hooded, sheltering the flower's reproductive organs. They flower from mid to late summer. Try 'Little Darling' (rose pink and yellow), 'Obelisk' (orange red), and 'Piquant' (black red).
- *Gladiolus communis* subsp. *byzantinus* (syn. *G. byzantinus*) (90 cm, 36 in.) is often available in mail-order catalogues. In mid-summer, this species produces up to twenty magenta, funnel-shaped flowers per stem.
- *Gladiolus callianthus* (syn. *Acidanthera bicolor* var. *murieliae*, *A. murieliae*) (90 cm, 36 in.), peacock orchid, is another popular gladiola species. Producing distinctly spearlike foliage, its flower spikes develop by early August, laden with buds that eventually open to reveal extremely fragrant, creamy white, star-shaped blossoms with throats of deepest mahogany.

Where to Grow

Tall gladiolas planted in small drifts (eight to ten corms) of a single cultivar make attractive vertical accents towards the back of mixed borders. Shorter varieties are charming toward the front of the mixed border; they also make excellent container plants. Gladiolas planted solely for cut flowers or exhibition purposes can be located in straight rows at the back of the border or incorporated into a vegetable plot.

Perfect Partners

Gladiolas most often approximate a natural look in the garden when planted behind shorter, bushy perennials, which soften their rather stiff, formal lines. Try asters, black-eyed Susans (*Rudbeckia* spp.), chrysanthemums, and monarda as partners. The rounded flower clusters of tall phlox cultivars paired with gladiolas is also an attractive combination. For a different look, plant a drift of gladiolas among low-growing shrubs with interesting foliage, such as spirea, potentilla, or dogwood (*Cornus*) species and their cultivars.

References

Addison, Josephine, and Hillhouse, Cherry. *Treasury of Flower Lore*. London, Eng.: Bloomsbury Publishing, 1997.

Bales, Suzanne Frutig. *Bulbs*. New York, NY: Prentice Hall Gardening, 1992.

Blair, Graeme J., ed. *The Efficiency of Phosphorus Utilization*. Armidale, Australia: University of New England, 1976.

Bonar, Ann. *Tulips*. Philadelphia, PA: Running Press, 1992.

Brickell, C., Cole, T., and Zuk, J., eds. *Reader's Digest A-Z Encyclopedia of Garden Plants*. Westmount, QC: The Reader's Digest Association, 1997.

Bryan, John E. *Bulbs*. New York, NY: Hearst Books, 1992.

Bryan, John E. *John E. Bryan on Bulbs*. New York, NY: Macmillan, 1994.

Burnie, Geoffrey, ed. *Bulbs for all Climates*. Sydney, Australia: ACP Publishing Pty, 1994.

Calgary Horticultural Society. *The Calgary Gardener*. Calgary, AB: Fifth House Publishers, 1996.

Casselman, Bill. *Canadian Garden Words*. Toronto, ON: Little, Brown and Company (Canada), 1997.

Cavendish Books. *Cavendish Plant Guides: Bulbs*. Vancouver, BC: Cavendish Books, 1997.

Coombes, Allen J. *Dictionary of Plant Names*. Portland, OR: Timber Press, 1985.

Edinger, Phillip, and Lang, Susan. *Bulbs*. Menlo Park, CA: Sunset Books, 1998.

Elliott, Jack. *Bulbs for the Rock Garden*. Portland, OR: Timber Press, 1995.

Glattstein, Judy. *Bulbs for Formal and Informal Gardens*. New York, NY: Little, Brown and Company, 1994.

Glattstein, Judy. *Flowering Bulbs for Dummies*. Foster City, CA: IDG Books Wordwide, 1998.

Glattstein, Judy, ed. *Gardener's World of Bulbs*. Brooklyn, NY: Brooklyn Botanic Garden, 1991.

Green, Douglas. *Bulbs*. New York, NY: Macmillan, 1998.

Grimshaw, John. *The Gardener's Atlas*. Willowdale, ON: Firefly Books, 1998.

Hendrickson, Robert. *Ladybugs, Tiger Lilies & Wallflowers: A Gardener's Book of Words*. New York, NY: Prentice Hall, 1993.

Hessayon, D. G. *The Bulb Expert*. London, Eng.: Transworld Publishers, 1996.

Hill, Lewis and Nancy. *Bulbs: Four Seasons of Beautiful Bloom*. Pownal, VT: Storey Communications, 1994.

Horton, Alvin, and McNair, James. *All About Bulbs*. San Ramon, CA: Ortho Books, 1981.

James, Theodore, Jr. *Flowering Bulbs Indoors and Out*. New York, NY: Macmillan, 1991.

Langdon, Brian. *Begonias*. Chester, CT: The Globe Pequot Press, 1989.

Leatherbarrow, Liesbeth, and Reynolds, Lesley. *The Calgary Gardener, Volume Two: Beyond the Basics*. Calgary, AB. Fifth House Publishers, 1998.

Leatherbarrow, Liesbeth, and Reynolds, Lesley. *101 Best Plants for the Prairies*. Calgary, AB: Fifth House Publishers, 1999.

Lovejoy, Ann. *Seasonal Bulbs*. Seattle, WA: Sasquatch Books, 1995.

Martin, Laura. *Garden Flower Folklore*. Chester, CT: The Globe Pequot Press, 1987.

Martin, Laura. *Wildflower Folklore*. Old Saybrook, CT: The Globe Pequot Press, 1984.

Mathew, Brian. *Bulbs: The Four Seasons*. London, Eng.: Pavilion Books, 1998.

Mathew, Brian, and Swindells, Phillip. *The Complete Book of Bulbs, Corms, Tubers, and Rhizomes*. Pleasantville, NY: The Reader's Digest Association, 1994.

McDonald, Elvin. *The 100 Best Bulbs*. New York, NY: Random House, 1995.

Proctor, Rob. *Annuals and Bulbs*. Emmaus, PA: Rodale Press, 1995.

Proctor, Rob. *Naturalizing Bulbs*. New York, NY: Henry Holt and Company, 1997.

Ross, Marty. *All About Bulbs*. Des Moines, IA: Ortho Books, 1999.

Scott, George Harmon. *Bulbs*. Los Angeles, CA: HP Books, 1982.

Stearn, William. *Stearn's Dictionary of Plant Names for Gardeners*. London, Eng.: Cassell Publishers, 1992.

Sunset Books, eds. *Bulbs for all Seasons*. Menlo Park, CA: Sunset Publishing, 1985.

Toop, Edgar W., and Williams, Sara. *Perennials for the Prairies*. Edmonton, AB: University of Alberta, Faculty of Extension, 1991.

Van der Horst, Arend Jan, and Benvie, Sam. *Tulips*. Toronto, ON: Key Porter Books, 1997.

Ward, Bobby J. *A Contemplation Upon Flowers*. Portland, OR: Timber Press, 1999.

Wells, Diana. *100 Flowers and How They Got Their Names*. Chapel Hill, NC: Algonquin Books of Chapel Hill, 1997.

Williams, Sara. *Creating the Prairie Xeriscape*. Saskatoon, SK: University Extension Press, University of Saskatchewan, 1997.

Index

In this index, numbers appearing in Roman bold type (e.g., **25**) indicate main entries in the book; italic bold type (e.g., *135*) indicates photographs or illustrations.

172

178

Authors

Liesbeth Leatherbarrow and **Lesley Reynolds** are enthusiastic gardening writers with many years of experience coaxing plants to grow in the challenging prairie climate. They are the authors of the popular *101 Best Plants for the Prairies* and co-authors/contributors to two other best-selling gardening books. They live and garden in Calgary, Alberta.